By Special Request

ANTONIA
RIDGE

FABER AND FABER
24 Russell Square
London

First published in mcmlviii
by Faber and Faber Limited
24 Russell Square London W.C.1
Printed in Great Britain by
Purnell and Sons Limited
Paulton (Somerset) and London
All rights reserved

Contents

Contents

Chaise Dieu – The Chair of God

I'd like to tell you about a village I know in France. It stands high in the mountain slopes of the Cevennes. There's a tiny railway station there, and the stationmaster, who is also the ticket-collector, porter, and everybody else official as well, solemnly puts on a fine peaked cap, and blows a trumpet to speed off the valiant little trains that four times a day pant up the mountainside.

And as you walk out of the tiny station, there, dark against the blue sky, towers a great abbey, houses, shops and cafés huddled close about it—the abbey and village of Chaise Dieu.

And as you walk towards the abbey the wind comes blowing down from the mountains, spicy, scented; indeed you will be walking on wild lavender and thyme and tiny pansies and heather. And there will be such a soft rustling and a whispering in the air that you will stop and wonder where the waterfall is. But it isn't a waterfall. It is the wind singing and whispering in the tall forests of pine-trees set all about Chaise Dieu.

Many eminent historians have written books about

this ancient abbey, telling how it dates back to 1045, when it was known by its Latin name of Casa Dei— the house of God. But time can do strange and touching things to names, too; and as the long years went by, this Latin name slowly mellowed down to Chaise Dieu —the Chair of God: surely the perfect name for this lovely, quiet place.

Inside the abbey you can see the most beautiful tapestries that tell the Bible stories in colours as rich and glowing as an orchard in autumn when the sun shines warm. And there are many strange and ancient monuments—a great pope lies buried here; and most singular of all, or so it seems to me, here in Chaise Dieu rests a Queen of England—so long, long dead— Edith, the Swan Neck, true wife to King Harold, who lost his life in the Battle of Hastings.

Running along the outer wall of the shadowy choir is a painting, or rather a whole line of paintings, oddly like the strip-cartoons now so fashionable in our news-papers. But these were painted five hundred years ago, straight on the wall, when the cement was still fresh and new.

Now five hundred years ago France was in a sorry state. The Hundred Years War had dragged to its miserable end, and everywhere there was ruin, famine, black desolation. And hard behind this cruel war came the Plague, wiping out whole villages in a night, laying waste great cities. And on the walls of the cemeteries and churches craftsmen, in their bitterness, began to paint terrible pictures of Death, dancing savagely among mankind, striking out at all who came in his path, the cruellest of assassins, the last enemy.

No wonder that these paintings were known as Danses Macabres—the Dances of Grim Death—for they were indeed most frightening, and merciless.

But here, on this wall of the Abbey of the Chair of God, an unknown artist, who thought more deeply than the others, painted a Dance of Death that was different, strangely different.

The colours, for instance—so gentle and faded, soft red and ivory, and a quiet cloudy yellow.

And there, in and out of a long procession of people, dances Death, a tall, thin, graceful figure, with the most expressive face.

First in the line stands a pope. We know he is a pope; on his head is the triple crown, the papal tiara. And Death, very quiet and thoughtful, stands behind him, and sets one foot on the pope's heavy gown that trails on the ground about him. And recognising that foot on his mantle, the pope stands still. He does not turn, but bows his tired head as if listening, as if asking, "Is it . . . you?"

Immediately behind the pope stands an emperor, a stately bearded monarch, wearing his crown. As Death sets his foot on the pope's cloak he also lays one quiet hand on the emperor's wrist. But surely this is no icy hand, for the emperor does not recoil; but very upright, he prepares to follow with regal dignity.

Then Death turns to a cardinal, a most melancholy prince, so melancholy that Death gives him a jovial

11

nudge with his knee, places his hand on his shoulder, and smiles as if to say, "Now, now! Why this gloom?"

Behind the cardinal stands a young King of France, looking so lost and worried, young head obviously aching under his heavy crown, that Death takes him by the royal belt and leads him along as you and I might lead a child.

Then on dances Death, eagerly greeting a knight, joyously taking him by the arm; gripping the hand of a bishop, before he meets a gentleman with a long sword stuck in his belt. And Death stops, and lays a hand on that sword, with a gesture that plainly says, "No, no, you will not need that. . . ."

And now Death meets a poet, a poet with both eyes shut tight, hands clutched as if in some last frenzy of inspiration. And without more ado Death takes him by the belt and leads him away as well.

Then he turns to a quiet nun, patiently waiting there, meek hands folded in prayer; but behind her stands a sturdy gentleman with a bulging leather money-bag hanging from his portly waist—a truculent merchant. And Death, suddenly very serious, puts one hand on his shoulder and points. "Sir," he seems to say, "I must ask you to go this way . . . with the others."

Then, with a swift gesture, he turns to bow to a great lady. And she puts her hand to her heart and turns her poor haggard face, as if catching the echo of other voices who also spoke fair words, who were also most kind and gentle.

But Death is full of surprises, for now he dances up

to a monk. And the good monk is staring at him, half smiling, half scandalised. For Death, if you please, is telling the monk a good story—oh, a most excellent tale, for he flings back his head and guffaws most mightily. "Can this be grim Death," thinks our startled monk, "this jovial companion, this best of good fellows?"

Then Death plays a little joke on a most elegant gentleman, a real fop—a "damoiseau", as they were called in those days—yellow hair curled about his head and buttoned into a tight jacket with long pointed sleeves, so long that the points trail on the ground. And the "damoiseau" is just about to put a rose to his nose to take a languid sniff . . . when Death suddenly whirls a noisy wooden rattle, and the "damoiseau" jumps and drops his rose. Then Death pats his hand as if to say, "Do forgive me! I simply had to gain your attention, my friend!"

Then on he dances, stopping now to tap a learned doctor unceremoniously on the head, now to lay a warning hand on the arm of a troubadour. The troubadour, not in the least put out, drops the lute which he has been twanging and turns to watch Death taking a great book from a studious monk. And the look on Death's face now plainly says, "Ah! These students! Heads forever in books!"

But now Death meets a poor peasant on his way to the fields, hoe over one shoulder, rough sack over the other.

As he feels the quiet arm of Death about him, he

turns, unafraid, unsurprised as if he knew that smile, as if he recognised a well-known friend.

Then Death stoops to touch a child; and stooping, puts one arm across his face, as if he knew that little children are sometimes afraid of a strange face. But the child, hands very still on his breast, gravely turns toward him, trusting—no shadow of doubt or fear on his little face.

Then Death gently plucks at the skirts of the young mother, and at last turns, facing the world, one arm again across his face—as if he knew that we too are so often afraid.

I cannot tell you how deeply these paintings moved me. And it wasn't only the homely people in them, who toiled and suffered and loved so many years ago. No, it was the poetry, the strange haunting poetry of Death, every movement so lovely and sure, that the artist must surely have drawn him in a white ecstasy of conviction, every stroke crying aloud what he felt in his heart, in his mind.

To him Death was no mean killer, no cruel assassin. Death uses no weapons, no violence of any kind. Death invites . . . points . . . leads the way.

To where?

Well, all I know is that the child turns to him in confidence, and that the peasant, so close to the earth, quietly accepts him, as if he knew, with Saint John, that he would "pass from Death into Life".

Chaise Dieu – The Chair of God

And I remember walking out into the warm sunshine very grateful to feel the air on my face; to see the wild lavender, the thyme, the little pansies and the heather; and to hear the wind still dancing and whispering in the tall pine-trees. And as I walked on in all this scented loveliness I remembered something a poet once wrote, something most comforting:

My name is Death . . . the last best friend am I.

TALES OF SAINT ETIENNE

1. Fireworks in Saint Etienne!

A Stéphanois is a native of Saint Etienne, and all true Stéphanois are gifted talkers. At times, when they consider a subject is worth it, they are also gifted listeners.

For instance, my old friend Leger Padde has never set foot in England, but he listens religiously to a programme broadcast in French called "Life in London". And many a time have I let my coffee grow cold before me, positively spellbound by Leger's subsequent reflections on life among the English.

"Take this Guy Faw-kes of yours," he said to me one evening early in November.

"Guy Faw-kes? Ah yes," I said, "Guy Fawkes."

"Precisely," said Leger. "Now I find I have a certain sympathy for that incendiary gentleman. And not only because I, too, in my time have yearned to blow up many a parliament. No, when I listened to his remarkable story last night I found myself remembering a certain incident in my own explosive youth.

16

Fireworks in Saint Etienne!

"I could only have been eleven or twelve at the time, for I was in the top class of my elementary school studiously preparing the Certificate of Studies.

"Oh, that Certificate of Studies! There were thirty of us in that Certificate class, all between eleven and twelve, and all being stuffed with studies from half-past six in the morning until six in the evening—with two hours off to eat at midday, of course.

"Yes, yes, our class began at half-past six sharp—and no excuses tolerated. And to tell the truth, once we were up and out we almost revelled in our hard lot. We felt important—grown up—as we clattered along the quiet streets in our wooden-soled boots, every boy in a sensible black overall buttoned down the front, black beret pulled rakishly over one ear, and every hungry one of us carrying his breakfast—a 'bichon' of good soup. A 'bichon'? Oh, that's good Stéphanois for an enamel or earthenware flask. Our mothers would fill them up; and as soon as we arrived we set them down on the top of the iron stove to warm up whilst we tore into our arithmetic. And when the younger boys turned up at eight o'clock, there we'd be, drinking our hot soup, very lordly and superior . . . seasoned scholars who'd been hard at it since crack of dawn.

"On the way home, however, we naturally sought a little recreation—down the alleys.

"Now don't tell me," said Leger with great severity, "that you, a citizeness of honour of Saint Etienne, have never noticed our alleys. Ask any young Stéphanois and he will tell you our alleys are the finest in France.

Fireworks in Saint Etienne!

They are those discreet passages you must have noticed between the houses—short cuts from one street into another—all very narrow, very silent, and pleasingly dark, even on the sunniest day. One feels anything might happen down our alleys, especially, of course, on a dark winter evening.

"Imagine, then, seven of us making our devious way home on this particular November evening, when suddenly Charles Blanquet said:

" 'Listen! I've got four sous!'

"Four sous! We stared at him. How, where did this capitalist in our midst get all that wealth?

" 'My feast-day yesterday,' said Charles, and jingled the sous in his pocket to prove it.

"Now the Feast of Saint Charles is on November 4th, so maybe it was an unseen but potent wave of sympathy that suddenly swept across the Channel from all those boys celebrating Guy Fawkes over there in England. But whatever it was, Charles Blanquet then said:

" 'What if I bought some crackers?'

" 'Crackers! Ah, chic!' we yelled, and flung enthusiastic arms around Charles and fondly pummelled him. And, still rejoicing, we swept him into a nearby bureau of tobacco which also sold crackers, three for one sou.

" 'Monsieur,' said Charles, with all the assurance of the big buyer, 'one dozen crackers, please. And could you spare me a match?'

" 'Certainly,' said the proprietor, and opened a box of expensive wax vestas and handed him one.

Fireworks in Saint Etienne!

"Then, carefully carrying all this, we set course for our favourite alley—the darkest tunnel of an alley with a vaulted roof. Your Guy Fawkes would have adored it. Moreover, our alley went one better than his coalcellar. It had the most sinister acoustics. A boy had only to go galloping through that alley, shouting as he went, and up and down, to and fro, would roll the echoes, as if some ghostly army had panicked and were stampeding behind him. In fact, a boy didn't relish going through that alley at night—not if he were alone. . . .

"But there were seven of us.

" 'Come on!' we shouted. 'Share them out, Charles!'

" 'No,' said Charles. 'I have decided to let off all twelve in one bang.'

" 'Mon Dieu!' we breathed.

" 'I have thought it all out,' continued Charles, very gratified to see us so staggered. 'I'm going to tie this cotton thread round them. I've soaked it in paraffin; and we'll put the crackers down here . . . no, there . . . yes, that's the place . . . and I'll lay the cotton along here . . . Now, the moment I set fire to this end you run like mad . . . in case we blow out some windows. . . .'

"And he struck his match on the rough wall, stooped, and set fire to the long trail of cotton. For one breathless moment we watched it flickering there.

" 'Run!' hooted Charles. And off we tore. As I told you, our boots had wooden soles, but the resounding clatter they made was suddenly drowned in an almighty BOOM—SW-ISH!

19

Fireworks in Saint Etienne!

"I tell you, no cannon, no thunderbolt ever reverberated better than that packet of twelve crackers. And that vaulted alley positively excelled itself! Roll upon roll of majestic thunder echoed and rang.

"But suddenly I was aware I was alone. All the others had fled. So I pounded on in the echoing darkness . . . straight into a pair of outstretched arms, and a voice that bellowed:

" 'Ah! So you were one of them, hein?'

"And I was clutched by two giant hands and marched out into the street. And when I blinked up . . . I almost suffocated. I had been captured by a policeman!

" 'Quick march!' he rapped and propelled me into the grocer's at the entrance of the alley.

" 'Madame,' he said to the grocer's wife, 'you heard that infernal din just now . . .'

"I looked at her in silent agony, beseeching her to be merciful.

" 'Din?' said that quick-witted great lady.

" 'But, madame!' cried the policeman. 'It must have shaken every window in the quarter.'

" 'Really?' said that angel of a grocer's wife. 'I think I am a little deaf at times.'

"The policeman led me out.

" 'Now,' he said, pulling out his notebook, 'we'll have your name and address. *And* the names and addresses of those other young rascals who all but bowled me over.'

" 'Monsieur l'Agent,' I implored, 'please, please let me off. I have to be home by half-past six. My papa . . .'

Fireworks in Saint Etienne!

" 'Your papa will be wanting his supper,' growled the policeman. 'And so do I! So we'll waste no more time. *Who were your companions?*'

" 'Please . . .' I blubbered. But it was no use. Like your poor Guy Fawkes, my courage gave way under the strain. Mental torture, in my case, of course. My papa never could understand why I required only ten minutes to go to school, and all of forty-five to come back home. And having dragged the names of my companions from me, did that policeman then permit me to gallop home? He did *not*. Still clutching me as if I were a candidate for Devil's Island, he and I then called on the parents of all six of my fellow-criminals.

" 'Monsieur, madame,' he began, 'I feel you should know that this evening your son, with six others, let off a considerable number of fireworks in a public alley. Under Section Six of Part Three of By-law 177, it is an offence . . .' and pa-ta-trie . . . and pa-ta-tra . . . till we finally made our dramatic exit, with both parents vowing to administer a sound correction, and warmly thanking Monsieur l'Agent for so indulgently overlooking the crime this time. And I'd pretend to be blowing my nose, so as to avoid the dirty look in the eye of each guilty party. No, I'll never forget that round of nocturnal visits.

"But that wasn't all. When we arrived at six-thirty sharp next morning, there stood Monsieur our Headmaster, waiting to greet us.

" 'Padde, Blanquet, Brunet, Lombard, Ginoux, Bertier, Pacoret—kindly advance to my desk! So you

21

are the seven young firebrands who let off crackers in the alleys, are you?'

"Yes, yes, our indefatigable policeman had also called on Monsieur our Headmaster.

"And Monsieur our Headmaster was a Stéphanois born and bred. By the time he'd finished talking, I saw all seven of us freezing to death in Siberia, or wherever it is they send the terrorists who all begin their life of crime by making law-abiding citizens jump out of their skins.

"Clearly, then, concluded Monsieur our Headmaster, it was his solemn duty to snatch us from our incendiary ways. And he paused to take solemn breath before pronouncing sentence.

"We were to remain in school every evening for an hour until we had completed—in our *best hand-writing*—all the tenses, all the moods, of the verb:

'to let off crackers in the alleys'.

"Only students of French grammar can know what this means.

"Hard labour.

"Hours and hours of it.

"The Present Indicative is brief enough.

I let off crackers in the alleys.
Thou lettest off crackers in the alleys.

He }
She } *lets off crackers in the alleys.*

We let off crackers in the alleys.

Fireworks in Saint Etienne!

You let off crackers in the alleys
They let off crackers in the alleys.

"The Past Indefinite is also concise.

I have let off crackers in the alleys.
Thou hast let off . . .

$He \atop She$ *} has let off . . .*

"Etcetera, etcetera. . . .

"But with the Imperfect one's heart begins to sink:

I was letting off crackers in the alleys.
Thou wast letting off crackers in the alleys.

$He \atop She$ *} was letting off crackers in the alleys.*

"And so on. And so on.

"But wait, oh wait, till the fevered student arrives at the treacherous pitfalls of the Subjunctives—the:

Oh, that I might let off crackers in the alleys.
Oh, that thou mightest have let off crackers in the alleys.

Oh, that { *he* *she* } *might have . . .*

"No, no," sighed Leger, "even now, after forty years, I still recall the penal servitude of that satanic verb.

"And so," said Leger, filling up our glasses, "let us drink to the health of that other unfortunate firebrand, Guy Fawkes! May he ever set off crackers in English alleys! And may all his tenses, all his moods, be merry ones!"

2. Davisky's Drum

There are two museums in Saint Etienne. One is just a museum. The other is the pride of a society, to which I belong, called "The Friends of Old Saint Etienne". And *our* museum is fascinating. All manner of oddments of days long gone. And among them a large and very dirty drum.

"Ah, that drum!" said Monsieur l'Abbé Dorna, when I asked him about it. (Monsieur l'Abbé is the President of the Friends of Old Saint Etienne.) "Now that belonged to Davisky, our great Davisky! He wasn't born here; he came here exactly one hundred years ago, all the way from Poland. Life was hard back there in Poland, and he'd heard there was a growing city in France, called Saint Etienne, where there was work for everyone in the rich mines and factories.

So one cold winter morning Davisky arrived in Saint Etienne; no money, no luggage, just the clothes he stood up in. He found a small room in the Rue Polignais, and the landlady looked at his eager young face and said, well, yes, she'd wait for the first week's rent till he found a job. She hadn't the heart to tell him times were also bad just then in Saint Etienne, mines and factories all on short time. She gave him a cup of coffee instead; and off went Davisky to look for work.

By nightfall he'd earned enough unloading potatoes to pay for his supper. But in the days that followed he'd often have gone to bed hungry if his landlady hadn't insisted:

"Share my soup. You can pay when things get better."

But things didn't get better. And one night Davisky came trudging home, shivering a little. Partly the cold; partly because the nail-factory where he'd been working a few hours that week had closed down, too.

As he turned into the Grande Artère he noticed a card pinned on a door, the door of one of our two dentists. There were only two dentists then in Saint Etienne. In those days people put up with the tooth-ache. If it grew too agonising they'd invite a sympathetic friend to help pull out the aching misery. Only if some obstinate molar refused to budge, no matter how they tugged, only then would they treat themselves to the luxury of a visit to one of our two dentists.

And here now was hungry young Davisky staring at the card pinned on the door of the dentist in the Grand Artère.

On demande un aide.
Help wanted.

He touched it. It was real. And he took a deep breath, climbed up the steps, and knocked at the door.

"Any experience?" asked the dentist.

Davisky smiled, and spread his hands in an exquisite gesture that implied a gift like his needed no experience.

The dentist stared at those expressive hands, the supple, wiry wrists.

"You'll do!" he said. "Week's notice either side. Eight sharp tomorrow morning."

And that was how Davisky became a dental-assistant. Soon, that dentist was warmly congratulating himself. Davisky was a find! He not only had wrists like steel, he had a remarkable gift for the dramatic. A sufferer felt he'd had his money's-worth when he saw Davisky joyously dancing before him, waving the tooth that had caused so many sleepless nights.

"Behold him! Roots strong as an oak-tree! One moment he is firm in your head, aching like hell; and the next . . . here he is, very quiet and tame! I will wrap him up. You must take him home to show to madame, your wife."

Yes, Davisky was rapidly making a name. And a name is always good for business. The dentist was enchanted.

So was Marie, his daughter, his pretty young daughter.

But the dentist was anything but enchanted when Davisky hung behind one evening.

"Monsieur, I must tell you I am in love with your daughter. And she with me. We beg your permission to marry."

"Marry!" exploded the dentist. "Marry a foreigner, a Pole, with no money behind him!"

Davisky's Drum

"Monsieur," said Davisky, eyes blazing, "I have more than money. I have brains! Adieu! I will return one day and ask you again. Only then I shall not come empty-handed. I shall bring a bank-book!"

This fine exultation, however, fell from him as he walked home. It was true. He had no money. He'd paid his landlady every penny he owed her. With the rest he'd bought an overcoat and a pair of forceps, beautiful shining forceps.

At the thought of his forceps his face shone again. And suddenly he took to his heels, and fairly flew home to his landlady.

"Madame," he said, "will you sell me a chair? I have decided to set up on my own."

Now every Sunday morning there's a busy market on the Place du Peuple in Saint Etienne. One can buy anything there from a canary to a set of saucepans. And the following Sunday morning, there, shouting with the best, was Dentist Davisky, warmly inviting passers-by to sit on his landlady's chair and get rid of the toothache.

But there, too, was a crowd of spectators, eagerly waiting for the yells. And this was bad for business. A prospective client was apt to forget the eloquence, the swift artistry; he'd only hear that yell. And off he'd slink, and decide to put up with his toothache.

Soon Davisky was tightening his belt again. But not for long. In Poland people didn't *go* to the dentist. The dentist came to them. Very well, Davisky would do the same. He'd become the first travelling dentist in France.

And he sold his overcoat, bought a little handcart, tied his chair on it, kissed his landlady, and set off.

From village to village he went, pulling teeth on the squares of a market-day, sleeping in barns of a night, saving every sou he could, and *learning*. Learning about people. Pulling teeth was simple. Pulling people —now that was an art that really did need experience.

Two years later, back to the Place du Peuple of St. Etienne came the experienced Davisky. But now he had a little platform rigged up on trestles. And on this platform was an armchair, luxuriously upholstered in green velvet; and a board fixed above it said in big capitals:

On arrache les dents sans douleur.
Teeth painlessly extracted.

To one side of the armchair stood Davisky in a scarlet coat, plastered with gold braid, feathered hat on his head. To the other side, respectfully stood his apprentice: his APPRENTICE. And a drum. A fine, shining drum.

No need to shout for an audience. People came thronging round. Then Davisky made a speech. He had returned, as a benefactor, to place his unrivalled skill and experience at the service of Saint Etienne. Extractions positively painless! Fees, equally painless. Threepence front teeth. Fivepence molars. And to celebrate this red-letter occasion Davisky would extract the first tooth of the day . . . free!

Up to the platform stepped a thrifty gentleman and gingerly sat down on the velvet armchair.

Davisky's Drum

"But, monsieur, pray make yourself comfortable," cried Davisky. "Lean back. Now open your mouth, and indicate the criminal."

And, still talking away, he whipped out his forceps; the apprentice walloped the drum, and out came the tooth. And if that gentleman yelled, nobody heard him. Indeed some swear that the sudden tintamarre of the drum, the torrential eloquence of Davisky were more effective than any chloroform. And far more entertaining for the spectators.

Soon business was flourishing. But Davisky went on saving. Three years he saved; and saved. Then, one lovely spring Sunday morning, when all Saint Etienne was out strolling, along the streets came a fine carriage, drawn by two superb white horses. And up on the driver's seat, in faultless evening clothes, waving his silk hat, bowing to left and to right, sat Davisky. And behind him, four gentlemen in scarlet uniforms, blowing bugles; with the apprentice, also in uniform, joyously beating the drum.

Down to the Place du Peuple they spanked and came to a magnificent halt.

And from that Sunday on, Monsieur the Dentist Davisky operated to *music*. Every sufferer solemnly mounted to the driver's seat, sat down, opened his mouth, and to the rousing strains of "Au Jardin de ma Blonde" out would come his tooth.

No patient ever knew if he shouted. It was for all the world like taking the leading part in a play—and a musical one at that.

Davisky's Drum

People began to flock from near and far to enjoy the spectacle: the white horses, the gay carriage, the spirited music, and the eloquence, the spell-binding eloquence of Davisky.

Presently, a plump smiling lady appeared at his side. Yes, Marie, the dentist's daughter. Davisky had kept his word. He had returned, with a bank-book, to claim his true love.

And she added a charming note of refinement to the spectacle. She used to tie a lace-edged towel round the necks of the lady-patients.

For years and years, every Sunday morning, the miners, the ribbon-makers, the weapon-makers of Saint Etienne would take their Sunday stroll down to the Place du Peuple to see and hear Davisky. He never disappointed them.

Other impertinent rivals, of course, began to imitate him. There was one, it seemed, up there in Paris. But not one of them could hold a candle to Davisky of Saint Etienne.

Then one Sunday morning the Place du Peuple looked strangely drab and commonplace. Davisky was not there. Davisky was dead.

Saint Etienne was stunned. One could not imagine Davisky . . . dead. Not Davisky.

They said as much in the speeches at his funeral.

"And they were right," said Monsieur Abbé Dorna. "For here I stand, still talking about him!"

And he lovingly patted the weather-beaten drum of Davisky of Saint Etienne!

3. Vive le Football!

S aint Etienne prides itself on being "très sportif". And I can bear this out. Many a time have I listened to wives and mothers over there bitterly complaining that all through the football season, for instance, their husbands and sons positively bolt the good Sunday meal they've taken hours to prepare, and, turning a deaf ear to all protests, off they gallop, come rain, come sleet, and cheerfully catch their deaths of a cold, standing there, rallying *their* team, the "Greens," on to victory. Oh no, the "Greens" of Saint Etienne don't lack encouragement and support, I can tell you. You can hear the roars of advice five miles away.

Then, still arguing, their supporters crowd into the tramcars again, and jolt off, packed like herrings in a barrel; arrive home hoarse and spent; and straightway switch on the radio, demanding silence, absolute silence, whilst they digest the sports review broadcast from Paris. And if this wasn't enough, those sportive gentlemen then tune in to London and listen to La B.B.C. telling them, in French, who won what, and by how much, over here in Britain.

31

Vive le Football!

Now one of the most eloquent, and certainly the most knowledgeable, of all these enthusiasts is my friend Monsieur Joseph Lanery. Moreover, other experts listen to him respectfully. And not only because he is a director of their football team. No! Who else in Saint Etienne can say, "Now, one of the best matches I ever saw in Britain . . ."

Yes, Monsieur Lanery, accompanied by Madame Lanery, once paid a visit to Britain. True, it was all of twenty years ago. But they remember it as if it were last Sunday. So do I. I'm the woman who arranged it all.

But before I begin to tell you about it, I must, in all honesty, make it clear that I have never understood football, nor why people get so excited about it. But nobody in Saint Etienne would ever have believed that. In fact, my own patriotic good sense warned me that I'd be positively letting Great Britain down if I didn't at least look interested.

So imagine me one sunny afternoon that summer of 1937 having a cup of coffee with the Lanerys and listening with patriotic interest to Monsieur Lanery telling me who kicked the decisive goal in our Cup Final in 1913, or something else remarkable. But when he paused for breath, instead of coming in with my usual "Ah oui, alors!" I heard myself saying, "Listen, you really ought to come over some time and *see* some British football!"

Monsieur Lanery spread both hands.

"And the business?"

Vive le Football!

Yes, the business. Monsieur Lanery is in the wholesale fruit-and-vegetable trade. He and his wife are up at crack of dawn every day, and up to then they'd never taken a day's holiday, except at Christmas and the New Year. Not that they couldn't afford it. No. There's just nobody handy capable of taking over.

"Well," I went on, in the easy way one always disposes of other people's problems, "what about Uncle Jules?"

Uncle Jules used to be in the business, too, before he retired and went to live in Avignon. Now if Uncle Jules could be persuaded to . . .

But Uncle Jules, it seemed, had never taken a day off himself, and didn't approve of people who did. He was hardly likely to be sympathetic.

So I said it was a thousand pities. And thought no more of it.

But Monsieur Lanery did. I hadn't been back a week before he sent me a telegram. It must have cost the earth, for it informed me that Uncle Jules had staggered the family by agreeing with me that Monsieur Lanery really should see some British football. And so he was prepared to take over for a week. *Next week.*

Monsieur and Madame Lanery were naturally seizing this golden opportunity, and they'd be arriving in London on Friday.

Friday!

And would I be very kind and arrange everything, tickets, trains, hotels, so that they could see as many first-class matches as possible—including, if it could be arranged, one match in Scotland.

I remember standing there, hair on end, reading and re-reading that telegram. In exactly five days' time the Lanerys would arrive in London, and I didn't even know if there *were* any football matches, much less where they'd be played.

And nobody I knew seemed to know either. I regret to say my husband, though sympathetic, was also precious little help, especially when he said: "If it had been *cricket* now . . ."

But I hadn't time to boil over. I had to *do* something. And at once! So I wrote, if you please, to the secretary of the Football Association itself. I implored him to send me by return of post (stamped addressed envelope enclosed) a list of the very best matches to be played anywhere in Great Britain the following week. I explained that Monsieur Lanery was a much-appreciated and most generous director of the "Greens" of Saint Etienne, and that he had the warmest respect, indeed affection, for British football—and that I would truly value his expert help in arranging a week's tour for this French football lover, especially as neither he nor his wife spoke a word of English.

Now Sir Stanley Rous doesn't know me from Adam, but whenever I see or hear his name I am still filled with real gratitude, for, thanks to the letter he so kindly sent me—by return of post—Monsieur Lanery had the week of his life in Britain. As for Madame Lanery—well, when he's happy she's happy.

Vive le Football!

So neither of them are ever likely to forget that first day: 18th September 1937. For on that day Monsieur Lanery, and Madame, of course, saw ARSENAL play.

ARSENAL

Best possible seats, of course. One doesn't realise the dream of one's life every day of the week. The match was Arsenal *v.* Sunderland. Sixty thousand packed spectators. But talk about orderly! Absolutely admirable. One felt the policemen on horseback at the gates were only there to add majesty to the scene. All the same, looking at those sixty thousand packed spectators, Monsieur Lanery was just remarking that even if one felt ill one couldn't possibly fall down, when out came some efficient-looking gentlemen carrying stretchers. Stretchers! Yes, they think of everything over in Britain.

Then Monsieur Lanery would hate to sound partisan, but he was naturally enchanted when Arsenal won 4–1. One would *not* like to go back to France and admit one had witnessed the defeat of *Arsenal*. And Monsieur Lanery especially remembers their centre-forward, a shooting star by the name of Drake. Absolutely formidable!

But what staggered Madame Lanery was the correct behaviour of the ladies sitting around her. The wives of the players, no doubt.

Now in Saint Etienne the wives of the "Greens" also loyally watch their Sunday match, but when some captious critics in the crowd grow restive and begin to yell such classic remarks as "Et là-bas! Don't take a nap again!" or "Mon Dieu! Kick the ball, don't kiss it!" . . . well, these wives don't take such innuendoes meekly. They have been known to turn savagely on the critics and hiss "Imbécile!" or make other searing comments.

But these English ladies—well, one couldn't tell if they were Arsenal or Sunderland. That will show you how correct they were!

The following day Monsieur and Madame Lanery took the train up to Blackpool. And as luck would have it, the chef of the hotel where I'd booked them a room, this chef could speak French. *And* he knew his football, too. So he took the day off, and personally conducted Monsieur and Madame Lanery to see Blackpool *v.* Brentford.

And after the match, which was a well-fought draw, 1–1, this obliging chef presented them to the secretary of Blackpool; and he introduced them to all the players, with whom they exchanged the most cordial of shake-hands and drank cups of excellent tea.

From Blackpool, Monsieur and Madame Lanery travelled on to Glasgow, up there in Scotland. And when they got there the sun was shining, the sky so blue, one would imagine it was Nice or Monte Carlo. And the receptionist at this hotel could speak French, and when Madame Lanery pulled off her thick coat and said, "Ouf! To think I thought it would be almost Arctic up here in Scotland!" the receptionist leaned over her desk and said:

Vive le Football!

"Madame, we usually have two days' summer in Glasgow. You're lucky. You're here for both of them!"

But to come back to serious matters. The match in Glasgow was Scottish League *v.* English League. And this simply could not have been better, for Monsieur Lanery had always understood that Scottish "footwork" was in a class apart. And it was! Those Scottish players had a way with their feet that was absolutely distinctive. Especially their over-to-you-back-to-me tactics. Oh, very swift and subtle.

And to make everything perfect, they won, 1–0. Again Monsieur Lanery would hate to sound partisan, but one wouldn't relish travelling all the way to Scotland to see the Scots defeated, now would one?

But that wasn't all. In that match, up there in Glasgow, on September 22nd, 1937, Monsieur Lanery with his own two eyes saw:

STANLEY MATTHEWS

Yes, the great, the famous Stanley Matthews. He was playing for the English League, of course. And Monsieur Lanery is not the one to boast, but he clearly remembers turning to Madame Lanery and prophesying:

"He'll go far, that one!"

And, mon Dieu, he most certainly has!

From Glasgow, Monsieur and Madame Lanery took the train and headed south again—to Wolverhampton. And the manager of the hotel there was also extremely helpful. He couldn't speak French but the head-waiter could. He was a Swiss. And that sympathetic manager gave this Swiss the afternoon off, and he went with them to the last match of that wonderful week: Wolverhampton *v.* Bolton Wanderers.

And that day those Wolves and Wanderers were all on their toes, and though there was many a palpitating moment, neither side scored a goal. Then, after the match, the Swiss escorted them over to meet the Wolverhampton secretary, and he introduced them to all the players. And again they had the honour of shaking hands with all twenty-two of them, as well as the referee.

And talking of referees, now that's something else that amazed Monsieur Lanery—the correct way British players accept a decision. Now in Saint Etienne one must admit one allows one's loyalty to get the upper hand. Even the kindest of spectators will bawl the most deplorable remarks about the referee's eyesight. And the "Greens" themselves, too, often speak their minds at the top of their voice. And then the referee, of course, vigorously answers back.

But a referee, over in Britain—well, he has a gentlemanly job, and no mistake.

And now, every time I go back to Saint Etienne, out comes the box in which Monsieur Lanery keeps all the souvenirs of that glorious week, and as we pass round the photographs of the players we relive each match all over again.

Vive le Football!

Mind you, I did once hear one insensitive visitor exclaim: "But didn't you even see the Tower of London or Trafalgar Square and those amusing pigeons?"

Monsieur Lanery looked at that feather-brained woman.

"Madame," he said, "me, I have no interest in towers and pigeons."

And he caught my eye, merrily lifted his glass, and cried:

"Vive! Vive le Football!"

4. La Retraite

Last summer a few of us were having a quiet talk and drink outside a café in Saint Etienne, when the clock in the comic little dome perched on the Town Hall began to strike eight. Now this clock is no ordinary clock. When it strikes eight, for instance, it booms a warning soh-me, and off it goes—doh, doh, doh, eight times doh. Then it obligingly repeats all this three times. But long before those twenty-four dohs had all sounded we were remembering the time when eight o'clock of a Saturday night meant something very special in Saint Etienne.

It meant "La Retraite"—the Retreat. I can't *explain* "La Retraite". I can only describe it.

The excitement began about a quarter to eight when more and more people would begin to collect on the square in front of the Town Hall. And wasting no time on unprofitable silence, they'd soon be hard at it, talking away, with every child in Saint Etienne able to dodge bedtime hopping and skipping between them.

It was the conversation of the *men* that fascinated me. They'd begin by explaining there had been no peace at home until they'd agreed to bring young so-and-so

40

along to see the Retreat. Then they'd roll another cigarette and off they'd go on that evergreen topic—the days when *they* were doing their military service. To listen to them, every man of them had done his two years in the finest regiment in France, where the discipline had been *infernal*. Name of a pipe, but they'd had it tough—chez-nous!

It was this "chez-nous" that tickled me. This useful French expression ought to mean "at our house" or "down our way" but at a quarter to eight of a Saturday night in Saint Etienne "chez-nous" meant one thing and one thing only—the crack regiments in which every man present had endured the most satanic of hardships. They had *standards* in those days. None of this sloppy, modern go-as-you-please business.

As for the military bands of those crack regiments . . .

"Chez-nous," would boast one gentleman, "all the musicians were professionals. None of your amateur oom-pah-oom-pah-oom-pah-pahs. From cornet to euphonium, every man in the band had his chestful of gold medals won at the Conservatoire de Musique—Paris, of course."

"Ah!" would rush another gentleman. "Chez-nous, the chef de musique was a CORSICAN!"

And we all knew what that meant. Boil over like milk at the drop of a hat. But did he have an ear, that Corsican! One false note, one microscopic note no other conductor would bother to notice, and out would fly his left hand, pointing straight at the offender. No need to stop the music. No need for words. If that

Corsican's left hand had four fingers extended, that meant four days C.B. Three fingers meant three days. And so on. And farewell to all rendezvous with one's sweetheart, for he also had a memory, that Corsican.

By now it was five to eight by the clock in the dome over the Town Hall, and we'd hear the steady tramp-tramp of feet. And on to the square would march the band of the regiment then stationed in Saint Etienne. Not playing . . . just marching, led by a giant of a drum-major. Immediately behind him marched "La Clique", drums and bugles slung on their backs.

"La Clique" were the young National Service men— mere amateurs with an ear for music, who could be trusted to come in, at suitable intervals, with an oompah-oompah on the bugle or a simple ra-ta-plan on the drum.

The *real* musicians, the professionals, marched behind "La Clique"—keeping their professional distance. As they say in Saint Etienne, one does not mix dusters with damask table-napkins—above all in a military band.

As if sensing this, "La Clique" always wore their kepis at the most defiant angle on their amateur heads. The more battered the peak, the more rakish the tilt, the better they liked it. Native genius, one felt, cocking a snoot at all this musical class segregation.

By now the band would be well in the centre of the square.

"Halte!" roared a voice.

The band snapped to attention.

La Retraite

"Repos!"

The band stood at ease.

And we all pressed nearer, admiring those glittering instruments, those impudent kepis.

One minute to eight.

Off went the clock: soh—me, doh—doh—doh . . .

But the rest of all those dohs would be lost in a roar of:

"Garde à vous!"

The band sprang to attention. And, believe it or not, so did we. The drum-major raised his stick and sharply brought it down again. A roll of drums filled all the air . . . louder . . . louder . . . and then broke sharply off as the bugles called loud and clear. We caught our breath, for the call they played was "La Retraite"— The Retreat, the old, old warning sounded for centuries past to recall all soldiers to barracks.

Then ra-ta-plan, ra-ta-plan, off went the drums again, and up on papa's back went young Benoit or Pierre, and off we marched. I say "we", and this is the simple truth. We all marched off the square, before, to the right, to the left, and behind that band. And as we turned into the long road that runs through Saint Etienne, six kilometres of it, straight as a ruler, the band would strike up a rousing quick-march—"The March of the Legion" or "Pan-pan-L'Abri".

And all the elderly sitting outside the cafés would leave their coffee, and games of dominoes, and stand up to see us pass. Others would crowd to their doorways, or hang out of their windows. And when the band struck up our favourite march—"La Sidi-Brahim", why, we'd feel as if we too were treading the sands of the Sahara as we hummed:

> *Forward, brave battalion!*
> *Jealous of independence!*
> *If the enemy dares to advance,*
> *Forward, ever forward,*
> *Death to the foes of France!*

And if an enemy had chosen that moment to advance we'd have made one mouthful of him. That'll show you what "La Retraite" did to us of a Saturday night.

And all this while the drum-major would be marching seven or eight steps before "La Clique", majestic as ever, in spite of all the youngsters cluttering up his feet, though naturally he'd mutter "Fichez-moi la paix là" from time to time, or threaten to put his boot behind them.

Then oop-la! Up would go his stick, and describe circle upon circle in the air, to the delight and admiration of the crowds now lining both pavements.

And the drums would take up, keeping us all in step as we turned a magnificent right angle up the Rue d'Arcole and into the Rue Mi-Careme, with all the traffic giving way before us. And not only because it was laid down by law that it was an offence to cut across a military parade. No, no. Saint Etienne had no need of a *law* to teach it to respect "La Retraite" of a Saturday night. And soon there would be a long procession trailing behind us, with the drivers of the tramcars coming in with their toot-toot-toots from time to time, half exasperation, half affection, and all the passengers leaning out to see that stick flying ever higher and higher, looping the loop in impeccable style to the measured roll of the drums.

Presently we came to our first halt—outside the house of the general of the division, and known to us all as "La Division". And this general would leave his dinner and come out on his little balcony with all his family and friends. And there they would stand, smiling with pleasure, as the band did its noblest with "La Marche Lorraine". (This general came from Lorraine.)

When it was over, he, and all his family and friends, would warmly applaud. And we'd applaud too, both the performance *and* the general. A good type, we told each other, hot-tempered but sympathetic. One *liked* him.

Then off we'd march again, drums rolling before us, tramcars tooting behind; and this time we were bound for the house of the general of the brigade, known to us as "La Brigade". And this general would also appear on his balcony with his family and friends and listen to the band swaggering through "Sambre et Meuse". Then they, too, would warmly applaud. And again we would applaud the performance, and then the general —but not quite so enthusiastically, I'm afraid, for this general of the brigade was one of those chilly, northern types, scrupulously fair, easy to respect, but somewhat difficult to *like*. And Saint Etienne likes to *like* people.

La Retraite

Then off we'd march again. And this time we were bound for the barracks. We weren't permitted inside the gates, of course, so we had to mass outside the railings, and watch our band march into the dark, waiting square.

There, they would halt. And not sparing themselves to the last, for us and us alone they would play "The Daughter of the Regiment" before they smartly dismissed and swaggered away into those drab, dingy quarters.

And we'd slowly turn and make for home. "La Retraite" was over. The papas would hoist Benoit or Pierre up on their backs once more, and take up their conversation all over again. But now there would be a different note in their voices . . .

"C'était le bon temps . . ."

Those were good days, chez-nous. One never had a sou to bless oneself with. But one was young. One hadn't a care in the world. Chez-nous . . .

Down the long road we'd straggle. By the time we came to the square again we'd have marched every step of four miles. But it was worth it. Next Saturday we'd all be there again, looking up at that clock in its dome on the Town Hall.

Where it still is, to this very day. But now when that municipal clock strikes soh-me, and eight times doh of a Saturday night, there is no retreat in Saint Etienne.

Only memories.

5. Place des Ursules

Nowadays the Place des Ursules in Saint Etienne looks like any other noisy French market-place. But as the French poet cries: "Where are the snows of yesteryear?" Where, for instance, is the Place des Ursules I knew and loved when I was a child?

I can see myself now, hopping up and down on the doorstep of my best friend, Eléonore Padde. Léo, we called her. And out she'd fly with her big brother, Leger, and behind them I'd hear their mother: "And mind you go to Vespers now!"

"Oui, maman; mais oui, maman!"and off we'd go across the Place de l'Hotel de Ville, up the Rue General Foy, across the Place du Peuple, and there we'd be —on the Place des Ursules.

We never asked what we'd go and see first. We knew. We visited the same sights Sunday after Sunday, as regular as clockwork.

First: Professor Hippolyte.

Now Professor Hippolyte always wore a white coat just like a dentist, though maybe not quite so spick and span, and he stood behind a little table on which was a large glass jug of water, an outsize toothbrush, and a pile of little boxes. And we'd wriggle our way to the front, just in time to hear the professor roar:

"Yes, I am Professor Hippolyte of the Faculty of Georgia, Kentucky and Virginia, so I am not the man to boast—a scientist is above such vulgarity—but I have spent the best years of my life perfecting the dentifrice that I now have the honour to offer to the citizens of Saint Etienne: Hippo-Dento, the fragrant tooth-powder made from the aromatic, tooth-saving herbs that bloom on the distant Alps!

"Ladies and gentlemen, if Hippo-Dento is not all I represent it to be, then treat me as an impostor! Chase me from this market-place immediately!"

And he would wait. And we would wait. But nobody ever came forward to chase the professor. And he would twirl his moustache, very haughty and sure of himself, and look round, till he spotted a suitable boy in the crowd.

"Here . . . you, my lad! Come here a moment!"

And I regret to say that we were always the ones who eagerly pushed the startled boy forward. We knew what was coming—he didn't.

"Ah, my lad," the professor would say, "let me look at your teeth! Tut—tut—TUT! When did you clean these last? WHAT? You don't know! Ladies and gentlemen, did you hear that? He doesn't know! Just look at them! Disgusting! Repulsive! Hopping with germs!"

And the professor would pick up his outsize tooth-brush, dip it in the jug of water, sprinkle some bright

pink powder on it, grab the boy firmly by the neck . . .
and soundly scrub his teeth.

"There! Saved! Saved in the nick of time by Hippo-
Dento! Smile, boy, smile! Show the ladies and gentlemen your teeth! Doesn't he look different! Why, the
boy positively sparkles! Moreover, his mouth is now
pure and sweet as the mountain air, thanks to Hippo-
Dento, the Friend of the Teeth, made from the flowers
that bloom on the Alps. Fivepence a box. Fivepence
a large box. Thank you, sir! Thank you, madame!"

But we'd see the boy edging his way towards us,
and there'd be a look in his eye we didn't relish, so
we'd take to our heels again and make for our favourite
seller of songs.

Now all the ladies and gentlemen who sold the latest
songs were over in one corner of the square. Most of
them had accordions or mouth-organs to help them out,
but *ours* had a little piano on wheels. Monsieur played
it with one hand, and beat time with the other; Madame
sang; and Mademoiselle, their daughter, went round
selling the copies.

"Now here," Monsieur would bawl—he had to, to
make himself heard—"here is the very latest hit from
Paris. Sent down by express, in fact. And we'll sing it
RIGHT THROUGH. We're not the sort who expect
you to buy a song after one verse. All we ask is that
you join in the chorus."

And he would strike up on the piano, and Madame
would begin to sing in her powerful voice; and after
a verse or two, there we'd all be, joining in the chorus:

Oh, he gives me orchids, so rich and so bright,
 But I'd give them all for a lily tonight!"
Or:

" 'No, dear comrade,' he said, as he sank in the foam,
 'You take the life-belt, you have two children at home.' "

Leger didn't like any sort of songs, but he'd wait
fairly patiently, and presently, fair being fair, we'd
tear ourselves away and go with him to see Hercule
and Partner.

Now Hercule was a wisp of a man with a thin brown
face, large mournful eyes, white flowing hair, and the
toughest skull in France. It must have been, for Hercule
would sit on the ground and invite us to gather round,
whilst his partner placed a full-sized paving-stone on
Hercule's head. I'm not exaggerating—it was a real
paving-stone all right. And Hercule, sitting there,
balancing his paving-stone, would burst into verse:

"Ladies and gentlemen, I promise you a treat;
 But even poor Hercule, well, he has to eat."

And when the ladies and gentlemen had thrown in
enough coppers, the partner would take up a great
mallet and—crack!—bring it down on the paving-stone.
"Come now, be generous," would pipe Hercule.

"Spare a few pence to buy us some bread,
 And he'll break this stone on my remarkable head!"

But I just couldn't bear to look. I'd screw my eyes
up tight, and I'd hear Hercule making up more and

more poetry, and his partner whacking away on the paving-stone, till crack—it was all over! The paving-stone would crash down in pieces, and Hercule and Partner would dash round rattling tin mugs before we all ungratefully vanished into the crowd.

After this we'd make for quieter, more highbrow entertainment. We'd go and see the Statues of Antiquity.

There were three of these statues up on a platform in front of a large tent, but they were only samples of the glorious statuary within the tent. At least that's what the gentleman standing up by the three statues used to say. He'd put a megaphone to his lips and roar:

"Ladies and gentlemen, you have heard of the mighty Acropolis in Athens: you have doubtlessly longed to behold the wondrous statues of antiquity. Ladies and gentlemen, you need not travel to distant Greece; within this tent, for threepence only, you may see all the gods of Ancient Greece . . . including Venus. Here, on this platform, you behold but three samples of our art —three warriors complete with swords and shields."

And we'd stare and stare at the three motionless warriors, in their white tights and vests, white plaster all over their arms, necks and faces. But they couldn't diddle us for long. "There! That one!" we'd shriek. "Look! That one! He's alive all right. You can see him breathing."

And the statue would give us a dirty look out of the corner of his eye, and the gentleman with the megaphone would lean down and hiss: "Here! Hop it! Hop it, you nasty little camels, or . . ."

Place des Ursules

We never waited to hear the rest. We'd be tearing over to the corner where Luigi of the Thousand Faces always stood of a Sunday.

Luigi stood behind a tall counter that hid all of him except his head and shoulders, and we'd push our way forward just in time to hear him say:

"If the honourable society will give me one moment I will present President Carnot."

And he'd stoop down behind his counter, and when he popped up again he'd be wearing a great square black beard and a mop of black hair and a terrific scowl; and the crowd would gasp "Ah!" and clap like mad. And the President would bow, and down he'd go, and up would pop the Czar of Russia, or the Emperor of the Turks, or King Edward VII or some other glorious unknown. But Luigi always reserved the star-turn for the end of course. He'd wait for silence, and then announce: "And now I will present to the honourable society—the MAESTRO PIETRO MAS-CAGNI."

And he'd disappear again, and from behind the counter would come the brassy strains of a gramophone —and before our eyes would rise the Maestro Pietro Mascagni, long white hair tossed back, eyes half shut, baton in hand. And the maestro would run his fingers through his long hair, tap the counter majestically with his baton, and with a superb gesture he'd begin to conduct a vast, invisible orchestra. Oh, you can laugh, but it always brought the house down—and a shower of coppers on the counter.

Place des Ursules

We hadn't an idea who the Maestro Pietro Mascagni was, of course, but we just knew he must be wonderful. After all—Mas-cag-ni. Why, the name itself was music. So different from the Durands, Frecons and Duponts of our everyday world.

Suddenly Leger would clap his hand to his head. "Vespers!" And we'd fairly fly over to the Church of Saint Louis—it's just across the square—and, well, if Vespers were nearly over we'd be extra fervent just to make up. Le bon Dieu, we felt, would understand.

Then we'd tiptoe out, and Leger would begin to jingle the three pennies in his pocket. And we'd say no, not chips, not sweets; we'd do as we always did—we'd buy some cakes. Now in those days a child could buy a pennyworth of broken cakes from any French pastrycook, but we'd make for the Place de l'Hotel de Ville and march straight into the warm palatial splendour of the best pastrycook in all Saint Etienne —with exactly threepence between us. And Leger would doff his Sunday hat and put on a shy whisper— we'd discovered that a polite timidity always paid handsome dividends—"Please, madame, may we have three-pennyworth of broken cakes, in three bags, please?"

And the lady in black silk with a gold watch pinned on her chest would smile benevolently on three such quiet, shy children, and disappear behind a bead curtain, and come back with three beautiful bulging bags.

"Merci, madame, merci!" we'd coo, and make our polite shy exit. But, once outside, we'd fairly prance back to the Place des Ursules, find a seat against a wall, and start on our cakes. Oh, such cakes, fit for a king, fit for the Maestro Pietro Mascagni!

And when we'd eaten every crumb we'd make for a nearby fountain. The Municipality hadn't risen to drinking-cups then, so Leger would take off his Sunday hat—a beautiful strong black felt—and he'd dent in the crown and hold that under the running water. And we'd drink in turn. And it was delicious. Not a bit like water at home. Then we'd dab his hat with our handkerchiefs till it was as good as dry, and then it would be time to go home.

But on the way we'd manage a minute or so in front of the boxing-booth. And yes, most Sundays he'd be there, marching up and down on the little stage before the tent—great gloves on his fists, great muscles jutting out all over him, great gold belt round his waist. And we'd set up a yell: "Oo-oo! Bonjour, Monsieur Royon, bonjour!"

And he'd wave a lordly great glove, and smile, and everybody would turn to stare at us. Could it be possible that those three children *knew* this great boxer, actually called him by name? And we'd walk off, very stiff and proud, because we *did* know him. We knew him very well indeed. He was the plumber at the end of Leo's street.

And the glory of this, and our wonderful tea, and all the rest, would go with us, across the Place du Peuple, along the Rue General Foy, over the Place de l'Hotel de Ville—and all the way home. And here I am now, still remembering it, as if it were yesterday.

6. Tite of the Place Chavanelle

The Place Chavanelle is the vegetable market of Saint Etienne. I have old friends who live right on this lively square, and I dearly love to lean out of their kitchen window of a morning when all the air is full of the shouts and banter of the stall-holders, the clatter of carts over the cobble-stones, and the mixed pungent smell of vegetables, fruit, and great bunches of sweet herbs.

But when I was a girl the Place Chavanelle had something altogether distinctive. It had its own celebrity. It had old Tite.

Tite. A gaunt six foot of a man, thin as a rake, with great hands and feet, who looked as if he were forever struggling to grow a beard. Not that he was, of course. He just didn't bother to shave. Neither did he bother to wash—though there *was* a boy who liked to boast he'd once caught old Tite stooping over the fountain in the Rue Roannelle. And so help him, old Tite had scooped up a thimbleful of water in the great hollow of his hand—and splashed it over his grimy face!

But that boy could boast till the goats came home. Nobody believed this fantastic libel.

Tite of the Place Chavanelle

Fountains! Rue Roannelle!

If old Tite wasn't on the Place Chavanelle, then he'd be up the Rue Villeboeuf, of course; or down the Rue de l'Epreuve; or along the Rue Mulatière. Those three streets and the Place Chavanelle—nowhere else! They, and they alone, were Tite's little world, and no offer was good enough to entice him down any Rue Roanne, much less wash himself, and in alien waters, too!

No, if business was slack Tite might be seen "obliging" of a morning on the Place Chavanelle—lending a hand with the sacks of potatoes, the crates of cauliflowers or some such commonplace employment. But his real job in life—and one in which he positively specialised—was buckets of coal.

For three ha'pence a large bucket Tite carried coal from cellar to kitchen, or upstairs flat, for every moneyed housewife in his little world. But the moment he had eighteenpence in his pocket he knocked off work. And went straight to the baker's for his daily loaf—a long stale loaf, reduced to twopence.

Bread under arm, he then made for the pork-butcher and bought twopenny-worth of scraps of cooked meat, and twopenny-worth of something we call "bretelles" in Saint Etienne—the succulent crackling cut off a roast leg of pork, sliced into thin strips.

Then down he'd sit, his honest back against some sunny wall, pull out his clasp-knife, and enjoy all this with slow, solemn relish.

Presently, jingling the rest of his capital in his pocket, he'd set course again, across the Place Chavanelle, on his way to a modest establishment which in those days sold a notable red wine at threepence a good pint.

And to any housewife leaning from a window calling to him to come across, do, and bring up some coal—or to any lesser offer of employment—Tite would shake a resolute head and call back:

"J'ai pas faim"—I'm not hungry.

I remember there was one woman—a stranger to Saint Etienne, of course—who used to try to get round old Tite. She'd even call him "Monsieur!" or offer to double the price, till presently Tite, properly exasperated, would burst out:

"But I've told you. I'm NOT HUNGRY."

To Tite it was as simple as that. Hunger was the only legitimate reason for work—hunger *and* thirst, of course, for Tite was a true son of Saint Etienne and liked his wine copious, red and strong.

And when he'd lowered his last glass of the day Tite would take a digestive stroll, deciding on a place to sleep. In summer it might be a bench under a tree. In winter a warm cellar, or the stable of the old inn in the Rue Mulatière.

As for clothes—well, a man can only wear one outfit at a time. So Tite wore his battered hat, coat and trousers till they were honestly past what his clothes were meant to do—cover him. Then, with infinite dignity, he would accept another pair of trousers or a coat, but only if the offer was prefaced with a friendly:

"This any use, Tite? Doesn't fit my old man now."

But once decently attired again, Tite declined all further offers, no matter how well meant.

"Thank you, but I've got a coat!"

And there'd be an impatient look in his eye that plainly said:

"And what the devil would I do with another?"

There was, however, one startling and permanent detail of Tite's rig-out—his sabots—a monstrous pair of wooden shoes so capacious that we proudly estimated two normal feet would positively slop about inside each of them. Very practical, though: for in winter Tite just wrapped each foot in an old scarf before slipping on his sabots. And in summer his great bare feet had room to spread—and to spare.

Moreover, once on, Tite never tried to lift these sabots of his. He didn't *walk*. He "ground" along, making as much din as if he were dragging a couple of cannonballs behind him.

Now one bright Sunday morning something came over old Tite. Maybe it was the warm sunshine, or the birds singing away in the dusty plane-trees, but he suddenly decided he, too, ought to say a grateful word to his Maker. So he crossed the square, climbed up the steps of the church there, and pushed open the door.

The church was full, hushed, listening spellbound to the eloquent preacher in the pulpit.

"Imagine, then, the good saint," he was declaiming, "how gently, quietly, he now steals to the altar!" When clomp . . . clomp . . . CLOMP! Down the aisle clattered Tite, crashed down on the first empty chair, bowed his head, and silently said what he had come to say. Then up he rose and, looking neither to right nor left, "clomped" out again.

I, alas, did not see this. But I *know* it is true. I have it from the preacher himself—Monsieur l'Abbé Dorna—and from everybody else in Saint Etienne, for that matter.

And Monsieur l'Abbé Dorna also told me how a lawyer came to see him one day, absolutely tearing his legal hair. Our Tite, it seemed, had been left a nice little sum of money by a sister in America. She'd gone there years ago. But Tite, if you please, was fiercely refusing even to enter the lawyer's office, much less sign any papers. He'd even told the lawyer precisely where he could go—he *and* his satanic documents.

Tite was taking no money from anyone—not even a dead sister. The only money he wanted was that which he earned with his own two hands. And that only when he was hungry, of course.

Then there was a certain—well, let us call her Mademoiselle X, living on the Place Chavanelle in those days. She was rich, charitable, and discreet. And every winter evening, as soon as it was dark, she used to put a jug of hot soup on the sill outside her kitchen window. And Tite obligingly drank it up. In his way Tite was discreet and charitable, too.

Now nobody ever saw Tite drinking this soup— but we *know* he did, for one day the rumour went round the Place Chavanelle that Mademoiselle X had left a certain sum of money in her will to provide a place for Tite in the "Charité". The "Charité" was the home then for the destitute old people of Saint Etienne. Sometimes a pathetic procession of them would go slowly over the Place Chavanelle on their way to church.

And Tite must have heard this rumour, for from that day he never went near Mademoiselle X. He turned a stone-deaf ear to all her pleas to carry up her coal, saw her logs. And every winter night her hot soup slowly froze on her window-sill, untouched.

Then one morning one of Tite's customers went looking for him—along the Rue Villeboeuf, then down the Rue de l'Epreuve, and up the Rue Mulatière.

"Ah well," she thought, "he's on the Place Chavanelle."

He was. He was lying on some sacks in the cellar under the baker's.

"Tite!" she called. "Come on! Get up! You said you'd come early!"

But Tite didn't stir. He was dead, just where he would have wished to die, in the heart of his beloved little world—the Diogenes of the Place Chavanelle.

7. Rejoice and Wait

This story also comes from the smoky mining-town of Saint Etienne in France. And I had the rare delight of hearing it told by a well-loved old priest there—Monsieur l'Abbé Dorna.

Now, as everyone in Saint Etienne will be quick to tell you, there is no one in all France who can tell a story better than Monsieur l'Abbé Dorna. But to my mind this is the best story he ever told—though I don't suppose I should ever have heard it if the conversation hadn't drifted round one evening to the way we all *hurry* nowadays, never feeling inclined to wait for anything—indeed, feeling positively hard-done-by if we don't see results instantaneously.

"Oh, but that's nothing new," argued Monsieur l'Abbé Dorna. "In fact, now I come to think of it, we have an old story here that tells how our Lord set out from Jerusalem very early one morning, on his way to Galilee. In front of Him, so our story goes, walked his disciples—James and John. And behind Him trudged Peter, grumbling a little because he didn't relish getting up so early of a morning.

"Out through the Gate of Herod they went, and

took the rough track that straggled down the Valley of Jehoshaphat, and then on through the foothills of the Mountains of Ephraim. And as they walked Jesus would point out a distant field of corn shining in the morning sun, or a bright patch of flowers springing between the stones about the roots of some gaunt figtree. And He would weave stories about all this, each with a truth caught up in its lovely words like the golden honey in a flower.

"When the sun stood high overhead, they stopped at a well to have a cool drink. And Peter divided the bread they had between them, and they ate this with a handful of figs.

" 'Ah, well,' said Peter as he scooped up the crumbs, 'maybe this evening we will come to some friendly house where they will offer us a good supper.'

"But the rough track led on and on, and in all that desolate countryside there was not a soul to be seen, not a house in sight. And the sun began to sink, and the shadows of the sycamore-trees grew longer and longer, and still there was no sign of a house.

"Then John and James—they were walking in front, if you remember—turned a sharp bend in the road, and there at last stood a house, a poor little house, walls made of beaten earth, and surrounded by a neat little garden, so neat it was almost pathetic.

"For a moment they stood there in the dusk.

"Then, without a word, Jesus walked to the rough door and knocked. 'Come in!' called a voice, a woman's voice. So they lifted the latch and walked in. And there, by the fire, knelt the woman. She was holding a large flat loaf; she must have just baked it under the hot cinders, for she was brushing the ashes from it with a little bundle of twigs. By her side, on a three-legged stool, sat a young man, perhaps twenty years old, and he was carefully pouring milk from a stone jar into two cups.

"Very surprised, they both rose to greet the four strangers.

" 'We are on our way from Jerusalem to Galilee,' said Jesus. 'May we stay here for the night? We are very tired.'

" 'And hungry and thirsty,' thought Peter, looking at the hot loaf.

" 'Rabbi,' said the woman to Jesus, 'I am a widow, and this is my only son, Azael. All we have in the world is this house and a cow as lean, poor beast, as those which Pharaoh of Egypt once saw in a dream. But our cow at least gives a little milk. And today has been a good day for us. I had the chance to barter half her milk for a half-measure of flour. And as you see, I've baked a fine loaf of bread with it. Indeed, I was just saying to my son that it would easily last us two days. But now, why, we'll be truly glad to share it with you. We so seldom have visitors. Yes, this *is* a good day for us and no mistake.'

" 'Yes, indeed,' agreed Azael, and offered the two cups he had filled to Jesus and Peter. And when they had drunk he refilled the cups and offered them to James and John. And Peter noticed that by the time he had filled a cup for his mother there was nothing but a spoonful of milk left at the bottom of the jar for Azael himself.

"Meanwhile, his mother had taken the loaf on her knees, and, carefully cutting it into six, she handed each one a part. And when they had eaten every crumb, and given thanks, Azael went into the garden and put up a little tent made of camelskin. In it he spread clean mats of plaited straw, and turning to Jesus he said, 'Rabbi, both house and tent are yours for the night. Where will you sleep?'

"'Here, in the garden,' said Jesus. 'The night is kind and warm, as warm as your heart, Azael.'

"So Jesus and His disciples slept that night in the little tent in the garden, and overhead the stars sparkled in the sky and the quiet air was full of the perfume of myrtle and myrrh.

"The next morning, as soon as the birds called, they were up and stirring. And when they had thanked the widow and her son, Jesus and His disciples set off once more along the rough track to Galilee.

"And once again John and James walked in front of Jesus, and behind him trudged Peter, silent for once. But Peter was never the one to keep silent long. Presently he could endure his thoughts no longer.

"'Master,' he said, 'only a few days ago we sat in the Temple with You watching the people cast their offerings into the treasury. And when a poor widow threw in a farthing You turned to us and said she had given more than all the others—they had given but part of their wealth, *she* had given all the money she had.'

" 'Well?' asked Jesus.

" 'Lord,' said Peter, 'I must speak my mind. That poor widow and her son who sheltered us last night gave even more than their last farthing. They did without so that we might not go hungry to bed.'

" 'Yes,' said Jesus, 'yes.'

" 'Lord,' said Peter, 'my temper may be short, but my memory is long. Did You not also promise us that whomsoever shall give us a cup of cold water to drink, he shall not lose his reward. *Reward*—that was the word You used, Lord.'

" 'Well . . .?' said Jesus. 'What would you do?'

" 'I'd be more than generous,' said Peter. 'I'd grant them the best, the very best, that could possibly happen to them!'

" 'Wisdom speaks with your voice,' said Jesus. 'Your wish shall be fulfilled.'

" 'Now God be praised!' said Peter, face shining with relief, and he fell in behind the others, and they went on their way to Galilee.

"Now when the time came to return to Jerusalem, the weather was so hot and dry that they took a different road back, the one that turned left to the River Jordan, for they knew the water would now be so low they could cross over on stepping-stones. So they did not see the widow and her son Azael.

"But the following spring Jesus again set out for Galilee, and again James, John and Peter went with

E

Him. They took the same rough track down the Valley of Jehoshaphat, and then on through the foothills of the Mountains of Ephraim. And, as before, James and John led the way, and Peter walked behind Jesus. But this time Peter was for ever urging James and John to hurry, hurry! He grudged the very time they took to eat their bread and handful of figs. He didn't put it into words but in his heart he longed to see the miracle, *his* miracle. At every turn in the rough road he would say to himself, 'Now we'll see a fine house, fields of wheat, flocks of sheep . . . and Azael and his mother in the midst of all their plenty. . . .' But the sun began to set, the shadows of the sycamore-trees grew longer and longer, and in all that desolate countryside there was no house, no rich ploughed field, no fat sheep grazing. And when they turned the sharp bend of the road there stood the poor little house, empty, in ruins—the garden a tangle of bramble and nettles.

"Peter stood for a moment looking at all this. Then, choking with angry disappointment, he turned to Jesus.

" 'Is this the reward of kindness? This house? This garden? Both, both in ruins!'

" 'Peter,' said Jesus, 'do you recall what you asked for Azael and his mother?'

" 'I do! I have a long memory, Lord! I begged you to reward them most richly. I wanted the best for them, the very best.'

"As he spoke, they saw a shepherd hurrying along

the track towards them. But before he had time to greet them, Peter called, 'Shepherd, you must have known the widow and her son who lived here. Why did they leave their house?'

" 'Their cow died,' said the shepherd.

" 'What!' cried Peter, his face black as a thunder-cloud.

" 'No cow, no milk, of course,' said the shepherd. 'And the soil in that garden is so poor and thin, they well-nigh starved. Then they heard—indeed it was I who told them—that Ephraim needed help with the harvest.'

" 'Ephraim?' rapped Peter.

" 'Surely you have heard of Ephraim,' said the shepherd. 'He lives in the valley just across these mountains. He has vast fields, and fine flocks of sheep, and great herds of cattle. The richest man for miles around. And the most upright. I know. I am one of his shepherds.'

" 'So Azael and his mother had to leave their home and go to work for others?' rasped Peter, very harsh and bitter.

" 'What else should they do?' asked the shepherd. 'At least they could eat their fill there.'

"Peter made no answer, but turned away, and stared sullenly at the ruined house, the waste of weeds in the garden.

" 'My master Ephraim,' went on the shepherd, 'has lost his wife, but he has one child, a daughter who is the light of his eyes. And it grieved him to see her growing into a woman with no mother to teach her.

67

And in the days that followed he was greatly pleased to see how willingly she would sit with the widow learning to spin and weave. As for Azael, he worked long and hard, giving of his best, so that everyone praised him.'

" 'Excellent!' growled Peter.

" The shepherd looked at him. 'They who sow in tears often reap in joy,' he said. 'When all the harvest was gathered in, my master Ephraim stood one evening in the doorway of his house. And a sudden sadness shook him. He was growing old. He had no son on whom to lean. And his heart grew cold within him. To whom could he safely leave all his wealth and his beloved daughter? It was then that he lifted his eyes and saw Azael driving home a flock of sheep. And in the setting sun the young man seemed to shine—grave, strong and upright as a young tree. "Jehovah!" cried Ephraim. "Hast thou sent me a sign? Has this young man been sent to bless my house?" And, turning, he saw his daughter standing there, and knew the answer. Yes,' said the shepherd, 'no need for words. It was plain that she had grown to love Azael. And tomorrow they are to be married. Oh, I tell you Azael and his mother bless the day they had to leave this poor house. But I must give you their message.'

" 'Message?'

" 'We saw you toiling up this rough track, from high up there on the mountain. And Azael, who has the eyes of an eagle, recognised you. "It is the Rabbi!" he said. " The one who once honoured our house with his three

68

disciples. Run and tell them the good news. Tell the Rabbi I count on his blessing tomorrow." '

" 'We will come,' promised Jesus.

" 'Then I must run and tell the women to prepare beds for you!' cried the shepherd.

"As he hurried ahead, Peter caught Jesus by the sleeve.

" 'Master!' he groaned. 'I am poured out like water.'

"Jesus took his hand.

" 'Peter,' He said, 'my poor Peter! And with that long memory of yours it should have been easy to remember the words of the psalmist!'

" 'Which words, Lord?' asked Peter, very humble now. 'There are so many.'

" ' "Rest in the Lord," ' said Jesus. ' "Wait patiently for Him".'

" 'Yes, Lord,' said Peter. 'Yes, Lord!'

"And with his heart soft as velvet within him, he walked with Jesus, James and John—on their way to the marriage of Cana in Galilee!"

8. A Bicycle for Christmas

When we were in our teens, my friend Eléonore Padde and I were enthusiastic members of the only ladies' cycling club in Saint Etienne—the Friends of the Pedal.

You should have seen us, the Friends of the Pedal! Very tall bicycles with high handle-bars; straw hats anchored on our heads with elastic that went under our chins; long skirts modestly stretched down over our knees, also with the help of elastic, one end buttoned to the hem of our skirts, the other looped about our shoes.

But what a time we had, pedalling round the green countryside that lies all about the grimy mining-town of Saint Etienne! And the meals we put away, maybe with our feet dangling in some little stream, and the rides home under the stars, scorching along the quiet roads, singing away at the tops of our young voices.

And now, every time I go back to Saint Etienne Léo invites some of our old Friends of the Pedal round for the evening. There are still, thank heaven, a dozen or so of us left—comfortable middle-aged women now, of course. And when we've all hugged each other, and kissed each other on both cheeks, and told each other how well and how young we all look, Léo rushes out to the kitchen and comes back with a great pot of coffee; and another old Friend of the Pedal, called Lolotte, who is a rare hand at pastry, brings out her "specialité" —an enormous tart stuffed with raisins and some sticky delicious mixture with almonds in it, and there we sit, enjoying all this, and never mind about our figures, catching up with our news and talking of the gay days gone by.

Imagine us then, one evening last summer, sitting in Léo's little living-room, the windows wide open to the cool night air, still talking hard, though the Town Hall clock had long struck eleven.

And somehow or the other the conversation had gone dancing back to our first—our very first—bicycles. And Léo had opened a drawer and found a faded photograph of herself, or rather a photograph of her first bicycle with Léo just holding it up—well in the background.

"I'll never forget it," she said, "never! Because of our Albertine, you understand . . ."

We said well, no, we didn't understand. And Léo poured out more coffee all round and said, well, she was five years older than their Albertine . . . married now and living up there in Paris, and the mother of five, all boys, and lively young imps too, we'd be pleased to know, especially young Pierre-Paul.

And we said yes, yes, a splendid achievement, but what was this little mystery about Albertine and Léo's first bicycle?

And Léo said, well, when she was fifteen she had managed to scrape through her Certificate of

A Bicycle for Christmas

Proficiency of the Practical School of Commerce and Industry. And if we didn't believe her, there it was, hanging up there on the wall, framed by her proud maman and papa.

Better still, far better still, Papa and Maman presented her with a bicycle—the very bicycle in the photograph there on the table before us. Oh, it wasn't a new one, of course. In fact, those handle-bars were so high that she just had to sit bolt upright or she would have dislocated her neck.

But it *was* a bicycle.

And her sister, Albertine—Titine they called her in those days—Titine used to stand and gaze on it, lost in longing.

But Titine of course was expected to wait for her bicycle till she also reached the same ripe age and advanced level of scholarship. In those days one did NOT present bicycles to mere ten-year-olds only in their second class of the primary school. Ah no! They were expected to wait.

Titine, however, decided *not* to wait. But she had already learnt that it is often a waste of a child's breath and time to wait on economical parents. So on the first day of November she took her case to the very highest court. She went straight to the good Saints of Paradise.

From the first of November, in excellent time for Christmas, Titine lay in her bed and offered up fervent petition, imploring, badgering certain of the good saints to join their celestial voices with hers as she chanted:

A Bicycle for Christmas

"Please, I want a bicycle for Christmas. I want a bicycle. I promise I won't expect the little Jesus to put any other presents in my shoes. I won't even put them out. Because that is the only present I want—*a bicycle*. It needn't be a new one. A secondhand will do, but not so tall as our Léo's, because I'm only ten.

"Saint Paul, pray for a bicycle for me. Saint Christopher, pray for a bicycle. Saint Antoine, pray for me, pray for a bicycle. Please, please, a bicycle. Amen. AMEN."

Yes, Titine, you'll notice, had carefully chosen her saints—only the more travelled among them were requested to lend their sympathetic voices as she prayed for that bicycle.

Of course Papa and Maman let her pray. One does not discourage the devotion and faith of a pious little ten-year-old, even if she does pray aloud and her bedroom is next door to the living-room. One hesitates even to suggest that silent prayer is perhaps just as efficacious—not to a ten-year-old, who certainly has not realised that walls are so thin.

So all that November long, night after night, Titine loudly prayed herself to sleep. And when December came she took further steps. She pressed her guardian-angel into service. Yes, he, too, was called upon to lend his angelic voice.

"I will be good. You needn't bother to watch over me. Just pray for a bicycle for me instead, please. A bicycle for Christmas, please.

"Saint Paul, Saint Christopher, Saint Antoine, Saint Isidore, pray for my bicycle. Ask the little Jesus for a bicycle for my Christmas. Nothing else. Just a bicycle. A BICYCLE. Albertine-Louise Padde, Rue Michel Servet, of Saint Etienne, Loire, France. Amen."

On the evening of the eleventh of December Papa turned to Maman.

"Marie-Thérèse!" he hissed. "Marie-Thérèse! For the love of Heaven let us buy that child her satanic bicycle before I, her father, smother her in her pillows with my own two hands!"

Well, at crack of dawn that Christmas Day Titine woke up, and felt for the matches she had ready on the little table by the side of her bed. And, trembling with excitement, she struck a match and lit her candle.

And there, down there on the mat, were her best buttoned boots. And she hadn't put them there. No, no, she had loyally kept to her promise not to put out her shoes that Christmas, but there they were. And in one was a pump, a shining new bicycle-pump. And in the other a lamp, a bicycle-lamp. And on top of this lamp was a note, a beautiful, heavenly note:

Look on the landing

So she tiptoed out. And there it was, on the dark, draughty landing, a bicycle, just her size—HER bicycle.

And very gently she wheeled it into her bedroom and leaned it against her bed.

Then she pulled on her clothes and her long stockings and her boots, and buttoned up her thick winter coat and rammed a hat on her head. And she took the money-box from her chest of drawers, and took out all her money, every sou.

Then she blew out her candle and ran through the door, down the stairs, and out into the cold grey morning.

And Monsieur l'Abbé Dorna told Maman afterwards that he had the surprise of his life when she came tip-toeing into the church, so early in the morning, and obviously so very hastily dressed. But Monsieur l'Abbé did not say a word. He went on putting the final touches to the "Scene of Bethlehem" that he and the choir-boys had set up in one corner.

And it seemed that Titine tipped all her money into the little box, and took six tall candles, and set them all to burn in the great candle-holder before the Baby, smiling there in the straw.

Then she knelt down and folded her hands. "Merci!" she said. That was all. "Merci!" But it came straight from the heart.

Then up she jumped and fairly flew back through the door, back to her bicycle waiting there by the side of her bed.

Nor was this all.

At ten to nine that Christmas morning a chorus of shrill voices was heard coming along the Rue Michel Servet. And bang-bang-bang went the knocker till it must have been red-hot. And when they hung their heads out of the window there was all Class Two of the primary school of the Place Bert, every single girl, massed on the pavement outside, calling: "Dis donc, Titine! Fais-voir ta bicyclette! Montre-nous ta bicyclette!'

A Bicycle for Christmas

"Ah yes," explained Titine, "I told them to come."

"When? When?" demanded Papa.

"Oh, last Friday when we broke up," said Titine.

And she reverently carried her bicycle down the stairs, and allowed two of her best friends to hold it up whilst she fitted on the lamp and the pump. Then down the street she wobbled, supported by these two best friends, whilst the rest of Class Two danced on either side, rejoicing. And all the neighbours with their heads out of their windows, wondering what on earth the din was about.

And Maman turned to Papa. "Claudius," she said, her eyes bright with laughter and tears, "Claudius, we did well to buy that bicycle. I would never have forgiven myself if we had let her down—and in front of all those girls too."

But Papa pretended to be very hard-boiled. He said he supposed he could wait another month for his new false teeth. Meanwhile maybe those obliging saints might give a thought to his digestion. And had Maman noticed one little detail—just one small detail?

"That young lady never as much as said 'Thank you' to us!" he growled. Then he stooped and kissed Maman; and flung back his head, and laughed and laughed.

"Ah no," said my friend Leo, blowing her nose. "I'll never forget that Christmas. Never."

And we Friends of the Pedal, sitting there, said, "Ah no, indeed!" and blew our noses too.

Housewife's Prayer

*L*ord, *in the carefree days when I was young and had*
    time to read,
    I would stand, as it were, outside an open door,
And listen to poets singing loud and free
Of the vast white radiance of Eternity.
But now I am middle-aged and much tamed with domes-
    ticity
I have come round to thinking that one has to be a poet—
Or a young evangelist from America—
Thus confidently to hold forth on the great Hereafter.
And, Lord, I know, none better, that words are tricky,
    treacherous tools
To one so unpractised,
And that my verse is free to the point of anarchy;
Nevertheless, Lord, very humbly, here are my thoughts on
    Eternity.

Lord, as I see it, this is the way of it:
We, the housewives, cluttered up with the day-to-day,
Have precious little time to air our views
On anything much—least of all the Hereafter,
The Present being always with us, and indeed too much
    for us,

Housewife's Prayer

So that poets and young evangelists and other positive
  spokesmen,
Sounding brass and clashing cymbals,
Have all the say.
And, Lord, I grow cold to think
That of Your tolerant generosity
You may provide for us too
That Paradise so vociferously claimed by the dogmatic few.

Lord, if they be worthy, give them each their pearly gate,
Their vast and shining mansion
Where they may sing Your praises in satisfied state.
But from all palatial splendour,
From the magnificent and the ornate,
From all that smacks of glorious Technicolor,
Deliver us, the housewives.

Lord, we were not born thus—prudent and circumspect,
Once we were young and eager.
This craft of housekeeping might tame others,
But not us, we vowed, not us.
And blithely rolling up our gay young sleeves,
We plunged into our brave new world,
Planning so much—all this, and children too—
On so precious, so rare a little.
Youth was eternal. We were not afraid.
We would never grow cautious, middle-aged and staid.

Dear Lord, now we know not whether to laugh or weep
At the careless courage, the lofty confidence,
With which we took the leap.

Housewife's Prayer

But I will come to the point,
I will speak for all my sister-Marthas,
I will say:
Lord, consider our long, our life-apprenticeship,
Condemn us not eternally to sit with still and folded
  hands,
All our dear victories so hardly won,
Forever dead, barren, profitless.

Let our Hereafter be a warm fulfilling
Of the long, the relentless years
That have gone sweeping by, so full to overflowing
That we are amazed to wake one searching dawn
And find our golden youth has flown.
And we, too cumbered about much serving,
Too careful and troubled about many things,
To catch the last swift glint of its shining wings.

Lord look kindly on us, the Marthas.
We too have seen visions. We too dreamed our dreams.

And now, Lord, I will speak for myself alone,
I will be outspoken and bold,
I will repudiate all blue-prints for my Eternity,
I will cry aloud that they leave me cold.

And I will tell You, in all simplicity, my own celestial
  dream:
A quiet home set about with cherry trees
That all the birds of Heaven and I shall share,

Housewife's Prayer

Marigolds in the garden, and boy's love, and mignonette;
And within, all I have loved the most in my many homes
    on earth.
Dutch tiles around the hearth, very blue on white,
Great cupboards, smelling of lavender,
Windows opening on grass, a commodious kitchen,
A shining stove, sweet-tempered, clean in one soapy wipe,
And the wherewithal, the bounteous wherewithal
To express my not inconsiderable culinary skill,
No synthetic anything at all,
No cutting down of this, no leaving out of that,
But me, singing Glorias, baking my fill.

So that, day by day, I shall lure the cherubs,
The bright, the laughing cherubs,
To come tumbling through my kitchen door
To taste my heavenly, my celestial cakes,
And they shall climb my cherry trees
And carol shrill and clear among my birds
And come flying down to pick my flowers,
My strange and homely flowers,
And set them in jam-pots on my window shelf,
And ask me for stories of children I have known on earth—
Especially the naughty ones, the merry heedless ones,
Who were so sorry when tucked up in bed they lay,
And always forgot the very next day.

And presently when every cherub has gone straggling home
    to sleep,
Tight bunch of flowers in rosy fist,

Housewife's Prayer

And all Heaven, and Earth below, lie hushed and still,
Some guardian angel, returning late,
Shall lift the latch of my garden gate,
And come inside and fold his weary wings
Over the back of my great armchair.
And I shall make him tea, a strong and excellent
    brew;
Being much on earth, he will need it good.
And I shall let him be. And presently,
Reaching for another of my day's baking,
He will murmur, "There is much to be said for this un-
    orthodoxy."
And the scented air shall come drifting in,
And it will seem to me that all the skills I learned on
    earth
Are blossoming about me, most celestially.
And by and by, I shall make bold to say,
"Dear Angel, do you think it could be arranged . . .?"
And he, reading my thoughts, will nod his tired head.
As if to say, "Leave it to me."
And I shall leave it to him.

And one day, apron about waist,
Bustling, cheerful, I shall hear steps that I know,
Faltering, hesitating, at my door,
And I shall cry, "Come in, my dear ones, don't be
    afraid!"
"Why . . . Mum . . ." they will whisper, eyes dark and
    wide,
"Of course," I shall sing. "Come right inside."

Housewife's Prayer

Lord, if this Heaven of mine be sentimental,
And move even You to mirth,
Consider in Your justice our sober lot on earth,
Call then to great Gabriel, though laughing still,
Cry, "Ho, there, bright Angel! Give these housewives their
  will."

Monument to Peter

Ninety years ago an American writer, Mary Mapes Dodge, wrote a book for children called *Hans Brinker or the Silver Skates*. It immediately became a best-seller, and still goes on selling merrily to this very day.

The story is set in Holland, and ninety years ago writers believed in instructing the young as well as entertaining them, so Mary Mapes Dodge conscientiously wove into her story every single thing she knew—or had ever heard—about Holland.

Now the most edifying Dutch story Miss Dodge had ever come across was the one she called "The Hero of Haarlem"—all about a sunny-haired boy, of gentle disposition, who was carelessly sauntering home one night when . . .

"He heard the sound of trickling water! Whence did it come? He looked up, and saw a small hole in the dyke, through which a tiny stream was flowing! Quick as a flash he saw where his duty lay! Throwing away the flowers he had been gathering, he clambered up the dyke until he reached that hole, and resolutely thrust in his chubby finger. The flowing stopped!

83

Monument to Peter

"And all that long, cold night there he crouched, knowing full well that if he drew out his finger the water would gush forth again; the hole would become bigger and bigger, and a terrible inundation would ensue. And the city of Haarlem down there would be drowned beneath the angry waters!"

At daybreak they found him, still crouching there . . . still plugging that hole in the dyke with his finger—at least Miss Dodge says it was his finger. Other equally well-informed writers swear it was his *thumb*. But thumb or finger, they all agreed that boy saved the dyke, and so saved the citizens of Haarlem from drowning in their beds.

I well remember the first time I was introduced to this remarkable story. It was in an English reading-book called *Golden Deeds from Many Lands*. And when we came to this Golden Deed from Holland, every head in Standard Two turned to gaze at my sister and me. We had just come from Holland, and our mother was Dutch.

"A-ah!" said breezy Miss Bracey. "Now Priscilla and Antonia will already know this lovely story, of course!"

"No? Dear me!"

She looked so shocked that my sister, very nettled, suggested it might be brand-new—sort of happened after we'd left Holland. . . .

"Good gracious me, no!" cried Miss Bracey. "Why, I knew this story long before I was your age!"

And her voice implied she hadn't come from Holland either.

84

We fairly galloped home that day, I can tell you, and burst in, demanding to know why we'd been kept in the dark about all this—making us look so silly—in front of all those girls, too!

To our dismay, our Dutch mother said she'd never heard of any young Hero of Haarlem, and, more deplorable still, she refused to take him seriously.

"Plug a hole in a dyke with a finger! Now! Now! What is that for a likely story!"

"But he's in our new reading-book! With pictures of him doing it!"

"So!" said our mother, calmly dishing up the dinner. "Now eat, als U blieft . . . and no more argument!"

We looked at each other. Dismissing the only Golden Deed from her native land like that! And in a voice that plainly said, "Och! What will these English think of next!"

A nice way for a Dutch mother to behave! Better not tell Miss Bracey, of course.

But worse was to follow. That summer when we went to Holland for our holidays nobody else in our benighted family had heard of the Hero of Haarlem either! Not even our cousins who lived in Haarlem! More disconcerting still, they too chose to treat him as a prime joke.

"Plug a hole in a dyke with a finger. Och, what an onion!"

An onion is the Dutch for a ridiculous story.

Bad as all this was, it didn't shake us half as much as their wretched dykes. Now we came to look at them seriously they really were so very wide and thick. Roads ran along their flat tops. Whole streets of houses were built on them and the grass grew thick and green on their tidy, sloping sides.

And, said our argumentative cousins, even if that boy of yours—ours, mark you!—even if that boy had found a hole into which his finger just fitted, what about the other end of that hole—yards and yards and yards away? Even *his* finger couldn't have stretched that far. And the water would have gone pouring into that end, and the dyke would have got wetter and wetter. And suddenly down it would crumble, over would rush the water, and wash away hero, clogs, finger and all!

The merrier they grew, the worse we felt. It was bad enough their not *knowing* about the Hero of Haarlem, without all this explaining just why nobody could ever have done that Golden Deed set down in black and white, with illustrations, in our English reading-book. A fine thing to have to go back and report to Miss Bracey!

We said as much to our exasperating cousins.

They said they couldn't help it. And, anyway, if it was true, why wasn't it in *their* story-books—like Piet Hein who gave wotto to the Spaniards; or, better still, that lady in the besieged castle. Now that was a story if we pleased!

This lady, it seemed, had appeared on the battlements of that besieged castle and shouted down to the enemy that she was now prepared to surrender everything, absolutely everything, provided she could keep her best-loved possessions . . . just as many as she herself could carry. Nothing more!

"Done!" roared the delighted enemy. And rubbing their hands, they ordered the gallows to be rushed up, ready to string up their most hated foe—that lady's husband.

And you should have seen their faces when to the sound of trumpets the drawbridge was lowered and out from the castle staggered that resourceful lady, blazing with her best jewels . . . and, on her back, carrying—HER HUSBAND!

How was that for a Golden Deed to offer our Miss Bracey—positively twenty-four-carat gold—and guaranteed 100 per cent Dutch.

We glowered at them. To the pump with their brawny lady! Who'd want to believe in *her*! But it was no use. These thick-headed Dutch just couldn't understand why we *wanted* to believe in the young Hero of Haarlem—just wanted to *believe* in him, that was all.

We weren't the only ones to be exasperated. Visiting Americans, brought up on Mary Mapes Dodge, would come to Haarlem and eagerly look round for the young hero's statue . . . or his portrait in the Town Hall . . . or even a modest plaque fixed on one of those quaint dykes. Not a thing, not a grateful thing! More frustrating still, nobody could even point out that fateful dyke, much less locate the hole.

And it was no use protesting that the whole darn

world knew about the boy who'd saved their dyke, that his story was a juvenile classic in every civilised language under the sun . . .

"Except here in Holland," would put in those unco-operative Dutch. "And if you will please take a look at our dykes, you will see why."

Now the Dutch may be unimaginative sticklers for the truth, the whole truth and nothing but the truth, but they are also a kindly and tolerant race, who like to take their sober time in dealing with any awkward situation. Saint Paul would have felt at home with them. He, too, took the view that "all things should be done decently, and in order".

So, decently and in order, the city of Haarlem considered their non-existent hero. For ninety years they considered him. And to my mind this in itself was downright admirable.

I ask you, what would lesser cities have done? They'd have promptly cashed in on this ready-made, world-famous inducement to tourists with money to burn. Think of all the easy money they could have made . . . the souvenirs, the postcards, the Cafés of the Triumphant Thumb, the Restaurants of the Hole in the Dyke, the Hotels Hero of Haarlem! And all the trippery, and oh-so-profitable rest! Do you know of any other city that has ever turned its decent back on such a gilt-edged investment?

The Dutch half of me positively swells with pride when I ponder on all this.

Monument to Peter

Imagine, then, how I felt when I was in Haarlem last April, and my Dutch cousin Antonia said to me, "Ah, before I forget, tomorrow we must go to Spaarndam. You must see our Monument Peter."

"Monument Peter?"

"Now don't say you have forgotten him, the boy we used to argue about—the one you said saved the dyke! Ja, ja, now we have a statue of him in Spaarndam. A very fine statue."

"So?" I said, just as my mother had said it, all those years ago.

But nobody noticed the note in my voice. Too busy talking about something else.

Which was just as well, for the very next day we went to Spaarndam. It's not far from Haarlem—and a *very* Dutch village. Water, water, everywhere, and dykes to the left and the right, holding back all this water from the flat, green polders.

And there, on one of these dykes, stands the Monument Peter, the legendary boy known to millions, outside Holland, as the boy-who-saved-the-dyke. There he is, on one stone knee, plugging an artistic stone hole with one stone hand, good Dutch clogs on his feet, honest Dutch face upturned to the quiet sky.

But it was the words on that monument, the sober decent Dutch words, that set my heart singing:

Dedicated to our youth to honour the boy who symbolizes the perpetual struggle of Holland against the water

Monument to Peter

The boy who *symbolises* the perpetual struggle of Holland against the water!

Behind that story, so ridiculous to the Dutch, they have nevertheless had the vision to sense a shining truth. Mary Mapes Dodge, and all those other writers, had only wanted to pay their tribute to Holland's grim, ceaseless fight against the water. The longer the Dutch thought of it, the clearer it became. And the Monument Peter is their expression of gratitude. It may have taken them ninety years to think it all out, but I ask you, have you ever heard of anything more decent . . . more honest . . . more DUTCH!

Birthday in Holland

I've just come back from Holland. I'm planning a story with a Dutch background and I wanted to sort out all my memories on the spot, as it were. So I intended to roam round by myself, and on the way to call in on my Dutch cousins, of course.

So I dropped them all a card:

"Hope to be in Holland soon. Don't be surprised to see me walk in one day."

And I signed this vague warning: Antonia van Engeland.

There are quite a number of Antonias in our family, and to save time and bother we are known as Antonia from Haarlem, Antonia from Amsterdam, and so on. I, of course, am Antonia from England.

Well, back came a batch of welcoming postcards, but from Haarlem came a special message—written in English:

"We were well surprised by receiving your card. Now what is this good news, hear! Bed for you is ready. And of course on the 18th we expect you. Best greetings and feelings to all the family. ANTONIA."

The 18th. . . . I was clearly being told that I was

expected to turn up in Haarlem for the 18th. But why the 18th?

Then the light broke. The 18th is Antonia from Haarlem's birthday.

Now Antonia from Haarlem is my first cousin and much about my own age, in her sensible fifties. But in Holland a birthday *is a birthday*, and taken very seriously, never mind what age.

Other years I knew nobody thought the worse of me when I forgot birthdays. After all I am only half Dutch, and the British, so admirable in many ways, are a casual race. Moreover, they all know I've lived for years in France, where birthdays are noticed even less.

But this year, there I'd be, in Holland—and I'd been reminded of the date too—so there would be no excuse. Not only that, I'm very fond of Antonia from Haarlem. I wouldn't hurt her feelings for the world.

So, on the evening of the 17th, well in time for the birthday, I turned up in Haarlem with my toothbrush and nightdress, and nice bunch of birthday flowers.

I was welcomed with open arms and a good square meal. The Dutch like their meals square. And over and over again, my cousin or her husband, Piet, would say, "Ja! Everyone's going to find it fine you here for the birthday."

Presently I gathered that everybody meant all the family within reasonable distance, not to mention friends and neighbours. Tomorrow it seemed I'd see just about everybody.

Birthday in Holland

"But tell me," I said, "how on earth do you all manage to remember each other's birthdays like this?"

"The birthday calendar, of course," said my cousin Antonia.

Now I'd completely forgotten the Dutch birthday calendar. It looks very much like any other calendar, a page for each month, pleasant pictures and so on; but there is no year marked on it, and each day has a good, large space to itself, ample room in which to write the names of all friends and relations whose birthday falls on that date.

"Oh yes," went on my cousin, reading my thoughts, "it still hangs in the accepted place!"

I laughed out loud. So did they. In nine Dutch homes out of ten the birthday calendar hangs where the family just can't miss seeing it—on the inside of the lavatory door.

Practical people, the Dutch.

And I cracked a mild joke, saying that I supposed when they made a new friend they said, "Now before we go any further with this delightful friendship, may I know your birthday, and do excuse me for a moment whilst I make a note of it."

But my cousin's husband, Piet, who takes everybody seriously, even me, roared, "Potvordikkie, no! Not so bluntly! Not so bluntly! We make discreet inquiries!"

Now my cousin and her husband, between them, run a small business, and the 18th was a Friday, and even in Holland you're not expected to shut the shop for a birthday. So in their case nobody would be calling until the evening, I was told, otherwise we would be keeping open house all day.

The moment we'd cleared away the supper things we put in the extra flaps of their large table, and put on the best table cover. By the way, the Dutch still go in for heavy red-velvet table covers, with bobbles all round them, the sort our grandmothers used to love. In the centre of the table we placed the bowl of flowers Piet had given his wife—lovely spring flowers most beautifully arranged by the florist. Then Piet brought out a couple of handsome boxes of cigars, a few boxes of cigarettes, and set them on the table, together with half a dozen ashtrays.

Then we saw to the tea-table. Now the tea-table stands in a corner of every Dutch living-room. It looks rather like a tea-trolley but built on more solid lines. On this we put the tea-light, the small heater on which the tea is set to brew. And in front of it we arranged the best cups and saucers, a little vase full of the best teaspoons, and a stack of small plates.

Then we ran out and gave a last-minute touch or two to the refreshments arranged on the kitchen table; made a very large pot of tea, set it on the tea-light; and sat down to wait for the callers.

"Listen," I said, "supposing you had to go away on your birthday . . ."

"One simply doesn't go away on one's birthday," said my cousin. "And if one is obliged to do so, one sends everybody cards to say so, of course, or telephones."

Birthday in Holland

I thought about this for a moment. Then I looked at all those waiting chairs, and the tea-table, all the best china, and my cousin in her best dress, and Piet in his best suit, and I thought of all the refreshments waiting out there in the kitchen.

"Listen," I said, "supposing they don't remember, supposing nobody comes. After all, you haven't *invited* them."

"Don't be absurd," said my cousin calmly. "Of course they'll come."

All the same, I went on feeling anxious. All these preparations, not to mention expense, for a lot of people nobody had invited, but who were supposed to remember it was the 18th and my cousin Antonia's birthday.

But I needn't have worried, for now the door-bell downstairs began to ring. Out went Piet and tugged the rope that opens their front door, and up the stairs came the first callers.

And for the next hour we did nothing but welcome them in. First of all, everybody handed my cousin a little gift: a plant, or some flowers, a pretty pinafore, a bottle of scent or a book they thought she'd enjoy, and as they gave it to her they all made a friendly little speech, wishing her health, happiness and good fortune, and asking the news of her two sons now overseas. And Antonia would thank them all warmly, and invite them to hang up their hats and coats; and then we'd settle them in chairs and pour them out a cup of the tea now simmering nicely away on the tea-light. And with this we offered biscuits, and Piet handed round the cigars and the cigarettes.

Birthday in Holland

By half-past eight the room was packed to the door. By some miracle we managed to fit everybody in round the table and there they sat, talking away fifteen to the dozen.

Everybody then had a second cup of tea and with this we passed round the chocolates. Funny combination, tea and chocolates, I thought, but the Dutch seem to like it.

Then out slipped my cousin and came back with a tray of glasses, and an enormous dish of cream-cakes. And Piet cried, "Now then, what shall we have to drink?"

The gentlemen all decided on a "borel"—small glasses of Dutch gin. But we ladies decided on something far more elegant, a smooth thick yellow liqueur made of yolks of eggs beaten up with brandy—at least I imagine it's brandy, but I'm no judge. And, believe it or not, on top of each glass was a thick layer of whipped cream. We didn't drink this, we tackled it with teaspoons. And I was told it was called "advocaat" —lawyer—because it had a way of mellowing even the most silent to eloquence. With this we served the cream-cakes. And when I say cream, I mean CREAM, thick, rich, generous and flavoured with coffee or chocolate.

Then up we rose, glass in hand, and burst into song:

> Now is it a birthday again, hoorah!
> You can see for yourself that it is,
> And we're all so glad to be here, hoorah,
> That's why we sing loud and clear, hoorah,
> Long may she live, hoorah,
> Long, long may she live!

Birthday in Holland

And with a final roof-raising hoorah we all sat down to sample the cream-cakes.

I looked at mine, all that rich, rich cream—that rich, rich, eloquent "advocaat". And, oh to blazes, I thought. Anyway, I could get something at the chemist in the morning.

So I got down to it with the rest.

Mind you, we didn't need the "borel" and the "advocaat" to set us talking. The Dutch dearly love a good round-the-table discussion. But they like to weigh their facts, to think before they give an opinion, so what they say may not be precisely sparkling, but it *is* sensible and tolerant.

But talking in any language is thirsty work, so presently all the gentlemen had another little "borel" and, oh my stars, when I looked down, there on the table in front of me was another "advocaat", and another cream-cake. And this time a gentleman who knew that both my cousin and I had been born in Amsterdam rose to his feet and gave us a song with a refrain that went something like this:

Omsterdom—yes, that's how they say it; if you say Amsterdam they know you're a foreigner. . . .

> *Omsterdom, we born on thy breast,*
> *Omsterdom, we love thee best.*
> *This word so small,*
> *Best loved of all,*
> *Omsterdom, O Omsterdom!*

Birthday in Holland

Now say the Dutch aren't a poetical race!

When we'd sung this through twice with great feeling, my cousin slipped out and came back with a great plate of thin slices of ham rolled up with a small slice of pickled gherkin tucked inside, and a little stick stuck neatly through it. I'd have liked a little bread with mine, but nobody else seemed to think it necessary.

And, of course, by this time everybody was feeling very warm and jovial, and the air was thick and scented with cigar smoke; and I happened to mention how startled I was as a child to see the tram-drivers in Amsterdam, steering the trams through the narrow streets and smoking a fat cigar. And somebody said, "Och ja! Those were the good old days, cigars twopence each, and Hitler bawling in his cradle."

That started an argument as to whether they *were* such good old days, and, if so, why hadn't we the sense to keep them that way—not to mention keeping Hitler bawling away in a nice, safe cradle. But my cousin evidently thought what we needed was a little more refreshment, so she nipped out again, and came back . . . with a dish of neat squares of cheese, good, rich Dutch cheese, and we all had a couple—just to keep us going.

Towards eleven o'clock a lovely smell of coffee drifted in, and in came my cousin again, this time with a great tray of steaming cups. And when I looked at mine, there, on the top, swam a lovely layer of rich, rich cream! But nobody else turned a hair, so I thought, well, if they can do it, rule Britannia, so can I! And I took a sip, and it really was delicious. I only prayed I'd think the same in the morning!

The coffee was evidently a signal that the birthday was drawing to its close. For one by one the guests now rose to their feet and said they simply must be going. And everybody shook hands with everybody else, and my cousin made a warm-hearted little speech thanking them all for coming, and they said they'd had a lovely evening—which indeed was true—and off they went.

And we set to work to tidy-up the room. And then to wash-up.

Oh, the washing-up! "No wonder," said my cousin Antonia, handing me the tea-towel, "no wonder our favourite joke is about the mother of a family, slumped in a chair, worn out, looking at the plates, cups, saucers, glasses spilling all over the kitchen, and groaning, 'Ah well, thank Heaven my birthday's over for the year!' "

But I said, yes, I supposed it did mean a lot of work . . . not to mention expense . . . but all the same, I thought it wonderful. All one's family and friends turning up like that—with such nice presents too.

"In fact," I said, now feeling very sentimental indeed . . . as well I might after all that cream, and the "advocaat"—"in fact," I said, "when I get back to England I'll start a birthday calendar myself."

And I have.

And it's hanging in the accepted place too.

Luilak!

I'm sorry but I can't think of one *single* English word that means exactly the same as the good old Dutch word—Luilak.

It means sluggard, loafer, lazy-bones—only more so. Somebody so bone-lazy that every decent energetic body longs to sail in and shake him up a bit.

You will gather from all this that luilak is hardly a polite drawing-room word. Yet come Whitsuntide, to thousands of Dutch children, particularly in Haarlem and Amsterdam, it is the very finest, the most exciting word in the whole Dutch language.

And on the Friday night before Whitsuntide they will do their very best to *prove* how much they cherish this remarkable word.

As soon as it is dark the fun will begin. All along the quiet cobbled streets the children will run, singing and shouting. They will stop at every door, ring every bell, rat-tat-tat on every knocker, rap on every shutter, shouting the age-old battle-cry, "Luilak! Luilak!" And just to show willing, they may even pause for a further insult, "Bedde-zak!"—Lie-abed! Lie-abed!

Moreover, the most thoughtful and enterprising

Luilak!

among them will have taken the trouble to devise other attractive ways of rousing their elders: empty kettles, old buckets, tin-cans and any other oddments that make a lovely din when walloped with a poker or stick.

Of course, there are, I regret to say, some mean-minded adults who have left their youth so far behind them that they will go to any lengths to put in a good night's sleep—even on Luilak Night. They will, for instance, unscrew and dismantle their door-knockers, or disconnect their electric bells. But the children will show 'em! To the fierce beat of kettle, bucket and tin-can, they'll voice their scorn of such shady dodges. Back will go their heads and the welkin will fairly ring with an extra ear-splitting "Luilak! Luilak!"

Now I was born in Amsterdam, and I still think Amsterdam the finest city in the world, but I have to admit—very grudgingly—that the children of Haarlem definitely put us in the shade on this particular night!

They have their Luilak Market!

This, if you please, is a flower-market. It opens at six o'clock on the Friday evening, and it stays open all night long, and all Saturday morning. And why? Because the sure, the certain way, to placate any angry Dutch mother is to walk in, a pleasing smile on your face, holding out, well in front of you, a nice bunch of flowers. That always does the trick. She fairly coos with pleasure, and promptly forgets all the things she has been saving up to say to you.

And keeping the market open all night long—now there's good planning for you! No need to dash off

101

just when the party's going well; no, you can choose your own time—when your voice shows signs of croaking away on you, for instance. Then off you run to the Luilak Market, buy a nice bunch of Mother's favourite flowers, streak off home with them, and, having made your peace, back you can gallop, refreshed and rejoicing.

Yes, you have to hand it to the children of Haarlem. They know how to make the most of their Luilak Night.

Moreover, it is claimed that it was they, the children of Haarlem, who first *thought* of this singular and delightful way of spending the Friday night before Whitsuntide.

This is the story they tell.

Long, long ago, in the sixteenth century, an enormous lake covered all the flat countryside between Haarlem, Leyden and Amsterdam. This great lake, having a circumference of some 44,000 metres, was very rightly called a sea—the Sea of Haarlem. And a very tempestuous sea it was too, on which great ships sailed, and fought, and sank. For in those bad old days Holland was waging savage war against the mighty power of Spain. And the people of Haarlem were second to none in the long bitter struggle for freedom.

Indeed, at one time the city could only count a handful of armed men. All the rest were away, fighting the Spaniards elsewhere in Holland.

The Burgomaster, a very sensible and cautious gentleman, realised that the enemy might get wind of this and send an army to surprise and capture the city.

Luilak!

So he engaged a watchman, called Lak, whose high duty it was to sit in a tall belfry and keep an eagle eye trained over the Sea of Haarlem. At the first sign of a Spanish ship Watchman Lak was to peal the bells and so give the alarm.

And here's the interesting point: the Dutch word for peal—to peal a bell I mean—is "lui".

Now at crack of dawn one bright spring morning, on the Friday before Whitsuntide, a band of children stole out from their homes and made for the sandy shore of the Sea of Haarlem—maybe to pick flowers, maybe just for the fun of chasing about in the crisp, morning air.

Suddenly one of them gave a shout and pointed an urgent finger. And there, against the pale sky, far, far across the grey water, sailed a line of ships, great, top-heavy ships—Spanish ships!

For a moment the children stood there, waiting. Came no peal of bells, no voice crying the alarm!

So, with one accord, they took to their heels, and flew back to the town, shouting "Lui, Lak! Lui, Lak!" And this, as you *now* know, means, "Peal the bell, Lak! Peal the bell, Lak!"

As they tore along the silent streets, those sensible children banged on every shutter, thundered on every knocker, tugged at every door-bell, and ever louder and louder rose the chorus, "Lui, Lak! Lui, Lak!"

Out from their houses poured the people, pulling on their clothes as they ran, crying on Lak to peal his bells. And presently, lazy Lak, fast asleep up in his belfry, heard the tumult, and seized his ropes and pulled and pulled. To and fro swung the great bells and pealed and pealed the alarm. And out from their beds sprang every man, woman and child in every corner of Haarlem—and prepared to meet the foe.

Oh yes, they prepared all right. For when the Spaniards landed, and stealthily advanced on the silent city, sleeping there so peacefully in the morning sun, they got the shock of their wicked lives—a roaring torrent of bullets, rocks, boiling oil and flaming pitch.

That taught King Philip of Spain to respect the good citizens of Haarlem, I can tell you.

Well, a lot of water has rippled under Dutch bridges since all this happened. The Sea of Haarlem, for instance, has completely disappeared. And don't ever ask what happened to it, because the classic reply is, "Oh, the Sea of Haarlem? We drank it."

The truth is, of course, that the Dutch have drained off all the water and reclaimed a whole new province, so that cows now graze on what was once the bed of that treacherous lake.

But the children of Haarlem have long memories. They're not going to let their elders forget that it was the children who once roused all Haarlem to face the foe. Not on your life! So here's more power to their voices, and long live the children's battle-cry: Luilak! Luilak!

Saint Nicholas of Holland

People outside Holland seem to think that the Dutch Saint Nicholas is just the same as the Santa Claus of other lands, twenty days too early, as it were. Not a bit of it!

Saint Nicholas of Holland is a very fine saint indeed. He wears a beautiful red cloak, stiff with embroidery of gold, wide gauntlet gloves set with sparkling gems, and a tall mitre on his snowy head, fairly blazing with precious stones. And no jingling round in a commonplace sleigh either. No, he canters round on a great white horse with trappings of scarlet leather choicely decorated with wrought gold. Oh, a magnificent saint, Saint Nicholas of Holland, I can tell you!

I'll admit there *is* a certain family likeness, however, between Saint Nicholas and the Santa Claus of other lands—the same long white beard, the same merry red face, and, above all, the same determination to give children a rattling good time.

But Saint Nicholas, being a true Hollander, is more prudent, more cautious. Behind *him*, on a coal-black horse, rides Black Piet, his devoted servant and friend.

Now Black Piet really is black, as black as night.

And it is his job to see that no Dutch child ever diddles that good Dutch saint. Nothing escapes Black Piet. He has eyes like an eagle. And talk about a memory!

"Och, your Holiness," he will say, "not all that for young So-and-so! Why, he's the lad who——"

And out comes something young So-and-so thought he'd got away with, something he thought nobody knew he'd done. And if it's just too awful, Black Piet winds up by saying, "No, your Holiness, take my advice, you leave one of my nice strong switches for that young feller-me-lad this year. That'll larn him!"

This, of course, is why all the pictures of Black Piet show him with a bundle of little switches (birches I believe is the correct English name), all ready to be used on the right spot, on the very worst cases. Not that Black Piet takes a delight in such extreme measures. No, he's a jovial soul who cheerfully hopes for the best, but—let it be understood—is also prepared for the worst.

Now I was in Holland some months ago, and they told me that good Saint Nicholas, like the rest of us, has his work cut out to make two ends meet these days. However, with the help of sensible Black Piet, he manages; and they both canter round with the presents as jolly and festive as ever. And every Dutch home prepares to receive them in the same good old way.

Now we always spent Saint Nicholas's Eve with my Dutch grandmother—Oma, we called her.

As we charged up the stairs to her little flat, out

would bustle Oma, calling to us to be sure and wipe our feet, and then change into our slippers, and to bring in extra chairs from the kitchen, and hurry-up-do because supper was on the table, and—potvordikkie!—one at a time please! And she wasn't deaf, so not at the top of our voices, ALS U BLIEFT!

In spite of the excitement we always managed to put away a good square meal, and Dutch meals *were* square in those days, and then, with Oma issuing orders right and left, we'd clear away the supper things, push the table back against the wall, and spread a dust-sheet all over the carpet. "Forty years I've had that carpet," Oma would say. "Better be safe than sorry any day."

No sooner was all this done than there'd be a loud ring on the door-bell. Down we'd all rush and open the door. There wouldn't be a soul in sight, but there on the doorstep would be three or four mysterious parcels. And no sooner would we get upstairs with that little lot than the bell would ring again, and down we'd scramble and find still more parcels on the step. This happened time after time, and never once would we set eyes on the people who left them. Even the hand-writing on the labels was carefully disguised. Nor did we find any straightforward messages *inside* the parcels, such as "With love from Uncle Jan". No, we used to find the most peculiar messages, often written in rhyme, which we'd read aloud to shrieks of laughter. And soon the dust-sheet on the carpet would be ankle deep in shavings and sawdust and paper and string, and everybody would be helping everybody else to guess who'd sent this or that; the more baffling the mystery, the more successful the present.

Sometimes of course it was quite easy—as on the night we all received a large white handkerchief, a cake of scented soap, and a poem which ran:

> *Oh, the spotless child with well-rubbed nose*
> *Is a pleasing sight, goodness knows.*
> *And great Saint Nicholas grieves to see*
> *Grimy hand and dirty knee,*
> *So gladden his heart this festive night,*
> *Use scented soap and handkerchief white.*

"Tanta Amalia!" we groaned in chorus. We knew! We'd had some. Always fussing about our hands and our handkerchiefs was Tanta Amalia!

By eight o'clock the bell would stop ringing, and Oma would say, "Come on, all hands to the clear-up!" And we'd set to work to pick up the paper and the shavings, and roll up the string, and brush up the saw-dust. Then we'd roll up the dust-sheet, and when everything was in apple-pie order again Oma would march us into the kitchen and hand us each a little bundle of hay. Now this hay was for Saint Nicholas's white horse. And, believe me, that animal has a most delicate stomach. He only eats the hay set down by good children. Nothing would induce him to nibble the hay of a really hardened sinner.

We'd take our hay, and solemnly set it down before our shoes which were arranged in a long line before the living-room stove. And then, with one accord, we'd burst into song. A grand old song it was too, in which we warmly invited Saint Nicholas and Black Piet to visit our house, begging them to bear in mind how hard we'd *tried* to be good, even if at times we hadn't been too successful, and ending up with all our warmest thanks for the presents we hoped we'd find in the morning.

And on this note of joyous confidence we went merrily off to bed.

At crack of dawn, or so it seemed to our elders, we'd be up and stirring. And, yes, our straw had gone. The white horse had eaten it up, every wisp. But our shoes had vanished, and the sitting-room door was locked. And with our hearts beating hard and fast, we'd wait till Oma came down, in her best silk dress, key in hand, and ceremoniously unlocked and flung open the door.

"Jé!" she'd cry. "If Black Piet hasn't put on my best cloth!"

And there, in the centre of the room, stood the large round table, resplendent in Oma's very best lace cloth, and on it piles of presents for everyone. And there, lined up against the walls, would be our shoes, bulging, overflowing with festive little parcels. And on top of every shoe a handsome letter in chocolate or sugar or marzipan—A for me, J for Jan, W for Wilhelmina, and so on.

Oh, I tell you Saint Nicholas takes no end of trouble to get every child the very things he most desires—within reason of course. And many a time does that thrifty Saint sit down and wrote a little note such as:

"Have noticed your skates are too small. Herewith one fine new pair. Kindly pass on old skates to Cousin Henk."

As for the rest of the day, that always sped by like a happy dream, with endless good things to eat and drink, and a festive litter all over the place, and nobody minding the muddle or the noise we made. In short, very like Christmas Day in other lands. Then in our family we had an ancient custom which allowed a child to stay up as long as he chose on Saint Nicholas's Day. And we did, of course. But at long last even we would call it a day. And presently all the house would grow dark and still.

But I'd lie in bed, listening . . . listening. And presently I'd hear it . . . the faint clop-clop of fairy horses carrying Saint Nicholas and Black Piet far, far away into the crisp December night.

Wedding in Holland

There was a wedding in the family when I was last in Holland, and of course I was invited. Now in Holland everybody *has* to be married in the Stadhuis—the Town Hall. If they are members of a church they can then arrange to be married in their own church or chapel, either on the same day or some time later. But the wedding in the Stadhuis must come first. Without a certificate to prove this no clergyman can marry them, no matter what denomination.

My invitation said that my niece, Antonia Theil, was to marry Hendericus Johannes Bolmers in the Stadhuis, Amsterdam, at eleven-fifteen on Friday morning. I turned up bright and early, and found a crowd of relations already waiting on the pavement outside. When I tell you that the bride's father was one of a family of ten children, and that they'd all turned up, with their husbands and wives and sons and daughters, all of whom had brought along their husbands and wives and sweethearts, not to mention the bridegroom's many relatives, well, you can imagine we were quite a party. And everybody was shaking hands with everybody else, and naturally there were a great many people

111

there who didn't know each other, so we all introduced ourselves in proper Dutch fashion. For instance, every time I came face to face with somebody I didn't recognise I'd say "Antonia Ridge, the Auntie from England", and he'd say "Piet van der Wal", and go on to explain exactly what relation he was to the happy pair. To add to the excitement, every now and then a wedding party would drive up, and we'd leave off shaking hands for a moment and surge forward, and then retreat, saying, "No, no, not ours!" And we'd all stand by, and watch that party walk into the Stadhuis. Arm in arm, two by two, they went, bride and bridegroom leading the way, everybody beaming and wearing white buttonholes; and this tickled me, all the small boys of the family, very clean and smart in "plus-fours".

Then from time to time a gentleman, in a blue uniform laced with gold, would appear and shout a number. And a line of cabs or taxis waiting on the opposite bank of the canal would set off, drive across the bridge and draw smartly up, just as a newly married couple and their families appeared at the Stadhuis door. Oh no, there wasn't a dull moment. We thoroughly enjoyed waiting for our bridal couple.

At eleven-fifteen sharp they arrived, and arm in arm walked into the Stadhuis. We all formed twos and walked behind them. We were shown into a very large reception-room and straightaway started shaking hands with the happy pair and all the relations who'd arrived with them.

Now, at the other end of the room was another happy couple who'd just got married; and all their relatives and friends were busily shaking hands all round too. Then another party poured in and they all started shaking hands as well; so the whole room was crowded with jolly people, all walking about, shaking hands as hard as they could go. Now I don't know one half of my many Dutch relations. After all, I haven't seen some of them for over eighteen years. However, I'm not the one to stand on ceremony, so I shook hands all round with the best. Mind you, I thought one or two of them looked a bit surprised when I announced I was their Auntie from England—and no wonder either! I'd got caught up in the wrong family! Luckily somebody spotted me and steered me back. Just in time too, for it was now our turn to form a procession and walk to the room where the ceremony was to take place.

At a handsome table in this room sat two gentlemen. The bride and bridegroom sat down on two chairs before the table, and we all sat down on rows of chairs behind them. One of the gentlemen then got up and in a sober quiet voice began to speak of the marriage vow the young couple were about to make, saying that it was a most solemn and binding undertaking. He then went on to talk of the duties of marriage, its joys and sorrows, and its ultimate triumph if they remained steadfast and true.

He then asked the young couple to stand up, the bride with her right hand in the groom's right hand. Their nearest relations were also asked to stand, and were asked if they gave their full and free consent to the marriage. Then, turning to the young couple, he asked if it was their solemn desire to wed. "Ja!" they said.

And taking up a hammer, he rapped smartly on the table and so declared them man and wife.

He then congratulated them, reminded them again of the solemnity of the vow they'd taken, and asked them to step forward and sign not only the register but a marriage-book. He then presented the book to them. Now this marriage-book takes the place of our wedding certificate, but it also has something more—twelve blank pages on which to enter the names and birthdays of the children. I gather that once you've filled up that little lot you can get another free—with hearty congratulations from the Dutch Government.

Well, the ceremony over, we all fell into line once more and walked back into the large reception-room; and, bless my soul, if we didn't start off all over again, shaking hands all round, and congratulating each other on another happy wedding in the family.

And then we all lined up once more and made our way to the door, neatly by-passing another large family party just making their way in.

Later on, when I said how startled I'd been to see so many couples getting married on one day, I was told I hadn't seen anything, that I ought to go to the Stad-huis of a Wednesday. On Wednesday it seems everybody gets married free, there's no charge of any sort. So Wednesday *really* is a busy day! So busy, in fact, that they get married in batches, three or four couples at a time! They all go in together. They all say "Ja" together, and with one rap of the hammer they're all made man and wife.

114

Wedding in Holland

And nobody understood why I thought this rather peculiar. "What difference does it make?" they argued. "They're properly married, aren't they? And free too! Which is more than you can do in some countries."

But if you can get married free in Holland, your silver wedding costs a pretty penny. You are definitely *expected* to celebrate. Usually your sons and daughters send a card to all relations and friends, which runs something like this:

"On the such and such date, our beloved elders, So-and-so and So-and-so, hope to celebrate twenty-five years of married life."

Sometimes a formal invitation to a reception follows, but it isn't really necessary. Invitation or no invitation, every evening for fourteen days before the happy anniversary every soul you know calls in turn to congratulate you. Yes, every evening for a whole fortnight Mr. and Mrs. So-and-so must dress up and sit waiting to receive congratulations and bunches of flowers, and gifts from all their relations and friends. And they, in turn, expect refreshment.

And well, as one tired woman said to me, it isn't only the tidying-up and washing-up when they've all gone home; fifteen days of this cost such a packet.

So I can't say I blame somebody in our family who sent round politely asking her friends and relations *not* to call, as she and her husband were going to celebrate their silver wedding by taking a quiet fortnight's holiday in Paris! Mind you, there was a lot of criticism. People didn't like it.

As someone put it: it simply was not *Dutch!*

Stories of Paul Harel

W hen I was in my twenties I lived for some time in the country, five miles or so from the town of Alençon in Normandy. And every now and then, in our weekly newspaper, I'd notice a poem written by someone called Paul Harel.

Now I liked these poems. They weren't clever or witty; they were the homeliest verses about the apple-harvest, or the good cider of Normandy, or a cart he'd seen lumbering along some lonely road with the farmer's boy, high on the hay, singing for joy at the top of his voice.

Then one winter's day I read a very different sort of poem. But this one, too, was signed: Paul Harel.

Outside . . . the fog, choking and white.
Inside my kitchen, warmth and light.
On hot embers, stew simmers, slow and deep,
Like some good saint, who snores in his sleep.
On the spit, fat ducks spin, crackling and spluttering;
In frying-pan, kidneys dance, sputtering and muttering;
On the grill, black puddings whistle and sing,
Sweeter than all the blackbirds of spring.

Stories of Paul Harel

Up to the rafters, the savoury smokes wing . . .
Outside . . . the fog, frosty and grim . . .
Dear Lord, I thank You that I keep an INN!

Keep an inn!

Why, yes, said my friends, didn't I know? Paul Harel kept an inn, the Inn of Great Saint Andrew, up there in the village of Echauffour. An old-fashioned place; been in the family for generations. And not exactly a paying proposition either. Every tramp in Normandy knew that the Great Saint Andrew was always good for a free meal and a shake-down.

As for Paul Harel, well, his poems weren't bad, but his cooking now! Absolutely inspired! I really ought to go there one day and sample it. And if Paul Harel took to me I'd probably sample his latest poems as well as his roast duck or his famous haricot-mutton. Not to mention his excellent stories. A gifted talker, Paul Harel, who dearly loved a sympathetic and appreciative customer.

And ten to one, said my friends, he'd be far too busy talking to bother to make out anybody's bill. And there was sure to be a couple of down-and-outs toasting their feet before his fire, blissfully eating him out of house and home as well.

And believe it or not, went on my friends, when somebody they knew once tried to talk sense to Paul Harel, what did that impecunious poet do but sit down and write another of his poems:

Stories of Paul Harel

From January to December, day after day,
To my inn men make their way.
Are they rich or greedy?
Good! I'll make them PAY.
Are they poor and hungry?
Oh, then Great Saint Andrew has all the say.
"Come in!" he cries. "Eat, and stay!
We're all Christians here.
We don't turn a brother away."

Naturally, after hearing all this, I made up my mind to go to Echauffour one day, and treat myself to a poetical meal at the Great Saint Andrew.

But I earned precious little, and there always seemed to be something of mine that needed mending. If it wasn't my shoes, it was my watch. Or my spectacles—I was forever breaking them.

But every time I saw another poem of Paul Harel's in the paper I'd promise myself, "NEXT pay-day I'll go to Echauffour."

And I'd picture myself sitting in the Inn of Great Saint Andrew—I wouldn't be able to rise to roast duck, of course, but there I'd be before my haricot-mutton, listening rapturously as the poet garnished it with fine verses and good stories.

Then, quite suddenly, I had to go back to England. And presently I had a letter from a friend in Normandy, and there, at the bottom of the page, was a hasty PS.:

"By the way, Paul Harel is dead."

Stories of Paul Harel

Paul Harel was dead. Now I'd never go to Echauffour; never see the Great Saint Andrew; never hear the poet sing of his Normandy; never hear his excellent stories.

Now this was all of thirty years ago. And I don't suppose I'd ever be talking to you about the poet-innkeeper who so captivated my youthful imagination if the sun hadn't suddenly started to shine one day in June.

Such a June! Sullen, cold, rainy. And it was just as dismal in France. My husband and I had spent ten chilly days there, and we were now on our way back, stopping a night here and there at any place we fancied. Then one morning, with no warning at all, the skies cleared, the sun came out, and all the countryside suddenly sparkled and shone.

And we bought bread and cheese and a bottle of cider, and turned up a lane, looking for a dry place to sun ourselves and eat a picnic lunch.

Now we'd chanced on a lovely lane. All along it grew the tallest daisies and buttercups I'd ever seen; and on either side fields, orchards and forests climbed gently up towards the clear blue sky. Not a soul about. Not a sound save the birds rejoicing to see the sun.

We were just finishing our bread and cheese, when I nearly choked where I sat.

"Look!" I gulped. "Look!"

And I waved to an old milestone I'd just spotted across the lane, an old milestone that said:

To Echauffour. 0.7 *kilometres.*

We were less than half a mile from Echauffour! I never covered half a mile so eagerly in all my life. And all the while I was explaining away, telling my husband about the poet-innkeeper, so hard-up, and yet never finding it in his heart to turn away a hungry man.

And when he could get a word in, my husband said, "Listen, thirty years is a long time. That old inn may not be there."

It was at this moment that we turned a corner and walked into Echauffour.

I can't explain it, but it was as if time meant nothing any more. The years rolled back; I was in my shining twenties again; I was in Echauffour.

Here was the quiet High Street, the trim little houses, the gardens gay with roses and marguerites, the old grey church, the peaceful convent. I recognised them all.

And that old house at the end of the road, roses climbing all over its walls, a yellow notice "For sale" pasted on one of its empty windows—that was the Inn of Great Saint Andrew.

"But how do you know?" asked my husband. "There's no sign outside."

How did I know! Hadn't I read about it in a hundred poems! And there, to prove it, against a wall stood a little monument:

TO PAUL HAREL
His friends and admirers
120

And as I looked and looked, a middle-aged man came strolling towards us, raised his hat, and said, please forgive him but he could see we were interested in the house and would we like to go inside? It wouldn't take him a moment to get the key.

I said, Oh yes, please! Nothing would give us more pleasure. As he hurried off, my husband, very alarmed, muttered:

"Here, go easy! He thinks we want to buy the place!"

But I didn't care. I was still asking myself if I wasn't dreaming, when back came the man, waving a great key. And unlocked the door, and flung it open.

"Very dusty!" he apologised. "Been empty so long. This is the kitchen, of course."

I couldn't believe my eyes. There was the great open hearth where once the flames had danced. There, tucked beneath it, was the wide, iron tray in which fifty plates at a time could be kept warm. And there, above it, was the spit, the old roasting-spit. And there, to one side, was the iron wheel that had sent it spinning round and round.

"He once wrote a poem about this very spit," I said.

"Oh, several," said the man. "But his favourite was the one that went:

Round and round,
Partridge, pigeon, duck went turning,
Round and round,
O'er clear fire burning.

Round and round
You sent them whirling,
Round and round
Forever turning.
But now your song is hoarse and spent.
'So old! So old!' you groan and lament.
'My teeth are broken. My wheel won't turn.
Leave me in peace. Let the darn dinner burn!'

'Wake up, old friend, wake up! Take a look!
It's lamb, old wolf, good lamb on your hook!' "

The man broke off, and gently patted the old roasting-spit.

"Monsieur," I said, "don't think me mad, but I could almost believe I was listening to Monsieur Harel himself."

"You are," he said. "You are."

We stared at him.

"I'm his son," he said. "Paul Harel's son."

"Yes," said the man again. "I'm his son, Paul Harel's son. So you have heard of him!"

"Why, yes," I said. "I used to cut out all his poems from the newspaper when I was a girl. It's like a dream, coming here, after all these years."

"Then you must see the table where he wrote," said Monsieur Harel.

We followed him across a stone-flagged passage and into another room with wide windows at either end.

"The dining-room," said Monsieur Harel. "You see,

these front windows look down the High Street. And these, over here, look out on the fields and hills."

"Just as in his poems," I said.

"Yes," said Monsieur Harel. "Somebody once said nearly everything of which he ever wrote lay in a circle of four hundred steps around our front door.

"And this old wooden table is the one at which he loved to sit and write. We hadn't the heart to take it away. It seems absolutely part of the old place itself.

"I can see him now, suddenly throwing down his pen and rushing to the kitchen shouting to take something off, that it smelled done to a turn; or flying to open the door to someone he had seen coming up the street. He dearly loved company. People used to come here from miles around—commercial travellers, farmers, insurance-agents, cattle-dealers, travelling dentists, pedlars, great writers from Paris . . . he made them all welcome, every one."

"And tramps as well, I believe," I said.

"Ah yes, madame. The Great Saint Andrew always had a couple of them tucked away in a corner. I expect you've heard of the most famous one, the tramp they called Little Road. No?

"Oh, all Echauffour knows about him. He started coming here when my father was a boy. He was called Little Road even in those days. Not that he was smaller than any other tramp. No. But he had such little eyes, very bright and kind; such a puzzling little smile; and he used to talk in such a little pipe of a voice. All this seemed to reduce him, as it were.

"And my father used to declare that people patronise an inn for a variety of reasons. They go to this one because they like good food. They go to that one because they're always in a hurry and they like to be served at the gallop. And the highfalutin go to yet another because they like a good white tablecloth as well as a good white wine.

"Little Road, however, came here, to the Great Saint Andrew, once a month regularly, for the best reason in the world.

"He never paid.

"My father said he once looked up his grandfather's old ledger. And regular as clockwork, once a month, there, on the debit side, would be: 'Little Road. One bloater, one mug cider, one small coffee, one tot brandy. 7½d.'

"Well, after ten years' credit, yes, ten years of bloaters, bread, cider, small coffees and tots of brandy, it was decided that the time had come to throw out a hint. Little Road simply must be asked to settle up, for now he really was working—odd jobs up there in the forests. And he had taken to turning up every day of the week for a meal.

"Little Road took the hint like a man. He fumbled in his pocket and pulled out an old notebook bound in pigskin.

" 'See this?' he said. 'Well, everything is written down in it. Every single sou. No need for you to worry. Everything's written down.'

"And with these reassuring words he carefully put

the book back in his pocket and walked out. And that was that.

"And all that winter long, day in, day out, on the first stroke of twelve, Little Road would come walking into this kitchen, holding out both hands to the fire, and smiling in turn at the tongs, the poker, and the grill—the grill where sizzled his bloater, his eternal bloater.

"And straightway somebody would hand him a great chunk of bread. And Little Road would deftly dig out a hole in this; and then taking his bloater, he'd cut off the head, shave off the tail, whip out the backbone, and bury it, piping hot, in the hole in his bread. Then he'd plug up the hole with the bread he'd dug out; and there he would sit, eating away with such enjoyment that just to look at him gave everybody else an appetite.

"Presently, when he came to the last crust, Little Road would ask in his little pipe of a voice for a small coffee and his tot of brandy.

"Then up he would get, face positively shining, and as he walked out through the door that little smile of his said, as plain as could be, 'Now, now! No carping about the bill. It will be all entered up. All written down. Don't worry about a thing!'

"Well, after thirty years' credit—yes, I assure you, thirty years' credit—my old grannie plucked up her courage.

" 'Little Road,' she said, 'you earned good money this week. You know you did. Now what about settling up?'

" 'Madame,' said Little Road, 'that is precisely what I have been doing.'

"He fumbled in his pocket and again pulled out his pigskin notebook. 'I spent the whole of last evening on it. I've caught up with every item. Every single thing is entered up. It's all written down, madame.'

"And such was his dignity, the old lady almost apologised.

"But after fifty years' credit—yes, I swear it, everyone in Echauffour will swear to it—after fifty years' credit my father himself plucked up courage, and had a word with Little Road.

" 'Paul,' said Little Road, 'you don't understand. You simply do not understand. So I suppose I shall have to prove to you that I am an honest man.'

"He pulled out the pigskin notebook. And this time he opened it and turned over the yellow pages.

"On every one was scrawled: 'One bloater, one cider, bread, small coffee, one tot brandy.'

"A thousand bloaters, ciders, bread, small coffees and tots of brandy.

"Half a century of bloaters, ciders, bread, small coffees and tots of brandy.

" 'There!' said Little Road, very pale and tense. 'There! Are you satisfied? Do I keep my accounts honestly, yes or no?

" 'Moreover, am I not a faithful customer? Have I ever been known to eat and drink somewhere else? Am I difficult about what I eat? Don't I finish up every crumb?

" 'And now you've seen my book, tell me, is everything written down, yes or no? Is my pen honest, yes or no?'

" 'Why, yes,' said my father, very ashamed to see poor old Little Road so upset. 'Yes, Little Road! Of course, Little Road!'

"Some time after that," went on Monsieur Harel, "Little Road fell ill. I remember my father at once took him a bottle of brandy.

"But he didn't even want to sit up and try it. We knew then that this was the end.

"Sure enough, that evening Monsieur le Curé went to the poor shack where Little Road lived and gave him the Last Sacraments. He received them very tranquilly, as if he knew he had nothing to fear from Eternity.

"And when the priest had gone, Little Road stretched out two old arms to someone unseen, maybe his Good Angel.

" 'Now, don't forget. Thank all those who have been good to me.

" 'And tell Paul Harel that if I'd had a field I would have left it to him. I'd have made him my heir.

" 'But, as it is, what with the price of boots, and a man cannot walk without boots, all I have to leave him is my notebook. Point out it is bound in good pigskin. Tell him he will see for himself. Everything is written down. Everything . . . is . . . written . . . down.'

"And Little Road closed his eyes. And died.

"Well, when the funeral was over, all the prayers said, my father sat here, in this very room, and with tears in his kind eyes looked at the old notebook, bound in good pigskin.

"And he turned to the last yellow page, and stuck on a stamp.

"Then he dipped his pen in the ink, and wrote across it:

Settled in full
Paul Harel.

"But forgive me," said Monsieur Harel, "I keep you talking here when I should be showing you round . . ."

It was then that he noticed my husband's face.

"Listen, monsieur," he said. "Don't look so un-happy! I know you are not here to make me an offer for the house. The truth is: I saw you both standing outside, and I gathered Madame was telling you about my father. I simply couldn't resist the temptation to have a word with you. I assure you it gives me the greatest pleasure to show you round the old place. So do come upstairs."

We followed him up the worn, wooden stairs, and into one bedroom after another.

"You see," said Monsieur Harel. "No modern com-fort whatever! Everything as in the days of Napoleon! All the floors so crooked! My mother was forever com-plaining nothing ever stood up straight, that all the furniture looked perpetually tipsy."

"But such lovely views from the windows," I said.

"Yes . . ." said Monsieur Harel. "But the trouble is, people also want taps with the hot and cold as well as views. In the old days, now, before all this hygiene, it was so much easier to keep an inn."

By this time we were downstairs again, and for no reason at all we had turned into the old kitchen once more.

"Yes, so much easier," sighed Monsieur Harel. "And so much more interesting! People had time to talk then! You'd be surprised at the gifted people who have eaten in this very kitchen.

"There was our Monsieur Bouche, for instance.

"Now he used to come through the door roaring like a lion. And everybody would shout, 'Ah, Monsieur Bouche!', and drop whatever they were doing to rush out and welcome him.

"You see, Monsieur Bouche may have been a traveller in wines, but he also carried a whole zoo-logical garden with him as well, an entire zoo—in his throat!

"He could imitate any living creature in forest, farm-yard, or sandy desert.

"He'd give the company anything they fancied: ravens at noon, blackbirds at dusk, the cry of a fox in the night, or pigeons cooing to the dawn.

"But his masterpiece was the jaguar. Now nobody in the Echauffour had ever set eyes on a jaguar, but that didn't matter. Monsieur Bouche's jaguar fairly froze the blood in every vein. And as the ferocious roaring died away, Monsieur Bouche would start from his chair and point to the ceiling. And from high up there would come the faint buzz of an invisible fly. Down, down, it

would fly, buzzing and buzzing, nearer and nearer.
And Monsieur Bouche would take a great swipe at it.
And miss it! And off would buzz that fly, sneering and
jeering. And then return, and hover most insolently
right over the table. And Monsieur Bouche would then
take such a swipe at it that the fly, frightened at last,
would take to his wings and streak for the door—
buzzing, buzzing, into the silence.

"Oh yes, a real favourite here at the Great Saint
Andrew, Monsieur Bouche.

"Mind you, he didn't *always* see eye to eye with my
father, for Monsieur Bouche declared himself to be a
free-thinker. When he remembered it, he'd even shake
his fist at the sight of a church. But my father always
maintained, however, that the good God would explain
everything one day to Monsieur Bouche, and that he'd
once had the most vivid dream in which he'd definitely
seen Monsieur Bouche entering the gates of Paradise,
cooing like a dove, to the delight of the angels.

"Yes, this old kitchen has seen some wonderful
evenings. There was one in particular that my father
never forgot. It seems that when he was a boy a
company of strolling players used to go the round of
all the market-squares here in Normandy. They'd rig
up a rough stage on a pair of trestles, sling a curtain
across, and pass round the hat before they gave a
performance. And an excellent programme it was, too.
All their plays had the blackest of villains and the most
spotless of heroines. Everybody very good, or very bad.
None of this insipid half-and-half stuff. And for good

measure, every now and then the villain would gener-
ously throw in a juggling act as well, or the heroine
would walk the tight-rope, or dance a pas-de-seul as
light as a fairy.

"Now one cold December night this company came
knocking at our door. A wheel had come off their van,
and please could they camp for the night in the field
just down the road which belonged to my grandfather.

"My grandfather said yes, of course; and then looked
at their blue, pinched faces.

" 'But come in first,' he said. 'Come in and warm
yourselves.'

"So they crowded in. There was room left round
the table for about six or seven. But twelve of them
squeezed in, not counting the children wedged in
between them.

"And they looked at the great fire burning there on
the hearth, at the roasting-spit, at the fowls crackling
upon it, the legs of mutton, the great pot of soup.

"And that good Christian, my grandpa, said, 'Well,
come on! Order! What's it to be?'

"They turned out their pockets. Barely sixpence
between them.

" 'Name of a pipe!' roared my grandpa. 'Don't keep
me waiting all night. Order, I say, order!'

"They looked hard at him. And decided to risk it.
They ordered soup, followed by a leg of mutton flanked
with a mountain of haricot beans. Then, to crown the
feast, at one end of the table my granny set down a

plate of cakes, at the other a dish of apples, and in the centre a beautiful cheese.

"And they washed all this down with jugs of good cider. Then my grandpa set coffee steaming before them, and a tot each of brandy.

"Their eyes shone. They smiled at each other. So must Heaven be, warm, welcoming, generous.

"Then my grandpa cried, 'Now it's your turn. What about a little performance.'

"They sprang to their feet and eagerly pushed back the great table. Everybody pressed against the walls—travellers, insurance-agents, servants, and the pig-dealer—every soul in the inn. And before their delighted eyes these strolling players seized spoons and forks and began to juggle. Up, up, to the rafters they sent them, wheeling and spinning, cascade upon cascade of forks and spoons, shining and glittering in the firelight. And all the while the children were weaving in and out, dancing on their hands, or turning somersaults as nimble as squirrels.

"Then, quite suddenly, abruptly, they too pressed back against the walls and began to sing, a strange and haunting melody. And a wisp of a girl began to dance. Like a leaf in the wind she danced, and every heart melted at the sight of her.

"And a dark strip of a boy seized a hat—it was the pig-dealer's hat, a very large one. And he made the round, holding it out. Soon the hat was full to the brim, as much as he could carry. Almost too much to carry.

"And the chief of the troupe took it from him, and turned to my granny, sitting there in her corner.

"And he poured it all out, every sou, into her lap. 'Voilà, madame!'

" 'But . . . but . . . it's for you!' she stammered.

" 'Ah, no, madame!' he said. 'Don't you remember? We are here as guests. Please divide it among the servants.'

"And he made a sign to the others. And they all bowed, and followed him through the door.

"And my father said they looked as beautiful as troubadours, as regal as kings.

"Yes," said Monsieur Harel, "this old house holds a thousand such memories. My sisters and I only wish we could afford to live here still, but it's too big. . . .

"We live in a cottage at the end of the garden. Won't you come and see it?"

We followed him through the back door, up some stone steps and across a small garden. And there stood the loveliest cottage, every wall covered with thick, well-trimmed honeysuckle in full bloom. And on a bench to one side of the door sat a pleasant, middle-aged woman shelling peas.

"My sister," said Monsieur Harel.

"Monsieur and Madame are from London over there in England," he explained. "But Madame once lived near Alençon, and she had heard of the Great Saint Andrew."

"Yes, indeed," I said. "And I dearly loved your

father's poems. I used to cut them all out of the news-papers. I assure you, it's a dream come true to be here at last, in Echauffour."

"But sit down, madame! Sit down, monsieur!" cried Mademoiselle Harel. "I know my brother when he begins talking. He never realises anyone is standing. But in his way he is paying you a compliment. He only talks to someone he senses is sympathetic. Not like our father. He'd talk to anyone."

At this moment Monsieur Harel came out of the cottage again, carrying a pitcher and glasses.

"You must taste our cider," he said. "It's good this year."

So we all sat down on the bench. And the cider was indeed cool and good, and overhead a thousand bees hummed in the honeysuckle.

"Yes," said Mademoiselle Harel, "we simply hate to sell the old place. But one cannot live on memories, now, can one?

"You know perhaps that even my father realised he simply could not afford to go on keeping an inn? Oh yes, he had to give it up.

"Just imagine, madame, on a Sunday for instance— of course, I'm talking now of the days when I was a girl —on a Sunday, he'd put on a meal that went like this:

> *Giblet soup, with dumplings.*
> *Tripe, with mustard sauce.*
> *Roast veal, beef, or mutton.*
> *Vegetables.*

134

Stories of Paul Harel

Fruit.
Cheese.
Cider, Coffee, Brandy.

"Second and third helpings positively encouraged. And all for two and threepence.

"We also threw in the bread as well, of course.

"No wonder, then, that the Great Saint Andrew was always full. Farmers, vets., doctors, writers, butchers, pig-dealers—there was one pig-dealer in particular; he could tell the weight of any living pig just by looking at it.

"Such talk, such arguments, such gaiety.

"And such appetites!

"The trouble was, my father was too much of a poet to be a good innkeeper. And too much of an innkeeper to be a good poet. Somebody once asked him what his output was that year.

" 'M'm!' said my father. 'Let me see . . . a couple of songs, an ode or two, and three sonnets. No better, no worse than the last batch.

" 'On the other hand, I've invented, or, to be more exact, I've improved out of all recognition two sorts of soup, and three—no, four kinds of stew. I've got one on this very minute. Come in and taste it!'

"Yes, that was our father. But, as I said, the day came when even he had to admit he was too hard-up to go on keeping an inn. So the sign came down. It was a beautiful old sign. It showed the head and shoulders of Great Saint Andrew. For well over a hundred years

135

it had swung there, on its iron bar, creaking in the wind. All Echauffour was desolated to see it go. But there it was. Bankruptcy was staring us in the face.

"Even when the sign was down, however, people still came knocking at the door. They just would not believe that the Harels no longer kept an inn. They'd sometimes knock us up at dead of night. And my father would hang his head from the bedroom window and explain.

"Eh! What! You no longer keep an inn? God bless my soul, I like that! Why, we've been coming here every quarter day, father and son, these seventy-five years. You're not going to see me catch my death of a cold out here all night, I hope? Your grandfather would turn in his grave if he knew of this.'

"So down would go my father and let them in. And if there was no other bed made up, he'd give them his own warm bed, and sleep in an armchair himself.

"But there is always a last straw. And it came one day in October, two whole years after the sign had been taken down.

"It was a lovely sunny morning. All the doors and windows were wide open. And my father was just saying how delightful everything was, so tranquil, so peaceful, when in through the open door marched a tall gentleman, silk hat on his head, brief-case under his arm.

" 'What time is lunch?' he demanded.

" 'Twelve sharp,' said my father.

" 'Good!' said the gentleman. 'And don't keep me waiting. I'll be here on the dot. And now, where does

Monsieur your Mayor live? I have to see him on legal business.'

"My father politely pointed out the Mayor's house; and down the street walked the gentleman.

"And my mother said, 'He's a lawyer, isn't he?'

" 'Yes.'

" 'But he thinks this is still an inn, doesn't he?'

" 'Yes.'

" 'Then for pity's sake be sensible! Send and tell him so before he comes back!'

"But no, my father wouldn't hear of it. What is more, he had two places laid in the dining-room. We always ate in the kitchen, of course.

"And as midday struck, back came the lawyer, and stood for a moment in the door, sniffing the air.

" 'A-ah! Smells good here!'

"Then he stalked into the dining-room.

" 'M'm, you don't seem to have many customers today. Let's have a look at the menu.

"'M . . . mm! Calf's head with vinaigrette sauce. Good!

"'Jugged hare! Splendid!

"'Roast pheasant . . . vegetables . . . apple-tart.

"'Fine champagne, 1804!

"'Heavens above! Is there a wedding here to-day?'

" 'No . . . no,' said my father, cool as a judge. 'Sit down, monsieur. I'm eating with you.'

"So they sat down, facing each other, and the meal began. My father gave him bumper helpings. Time and again he refilled his glass.

"Presently, the lawyer, very red and happy, said, 'This is a wonderful meal! You know your job all right. But you also know how to make people spend money, eh? If my wife could see me she'd scratch my eyes out. But she isn't here, so I'm not worrying. Time for that when I see the bill, eh, you old fox?'

"My father smiled, set down the coffee, and offered him a choice cigar.

" 'Monsieur Harel! Monsieur Harel!' sighed the lawyer as he sampled coffee and cigar. 'You simply must tell me what I owe you. Now I really *am* getting worried.'

" 'Calm yourself!' said my father. 'And give me your opinion of this fine champagne. 1804. What's more, I'll swear to it. Well?'

" 'La-la-la!' cried the lawyer and smacked his lips. 'An aristocrat—a real aristocrat!'

"Then his face darkened.

" 'But who d'you take me for? Rothschild? However . . .'

"He flung a banknote on the table. 'I had no intention whatever of spending this much. But you win. Take what I owe you.'

"My father pushed back the bank-note.

" 'No, thank you, monsieur.'

" 'Eh? What's wrong with it?'

" 'Nothing,' said my father. 'Nothing at all. It's just that I no longer keep an inn!'

" 'No longer . . .! Then why in heaven's name did you give me this meal?'

Stories of Paul Harel

"My father spread his hands.

" 'Because I enjoy a joke, monsieur.'

" 'Joke!' gulped the lawyer. 'Tell me, are you then a rich man?'

" 'No,' admitted my father. 'Definitely no!'

" 'I'm not surprised,' said the lawyer. And he threw back his head and laughed and laughed.

"Then he wiped his eyes and said, 'Wish now I'd brought the wife. She's young and pretty and she adores a joke. Pity she's not here too.'

" 'Oh, let's drink to her!' said my amiable father. And filled up both glasses with fine champagne, 1804.

"The lawyer drank his down in one gulp. After all, it was free.

"Then he got up, clapped his silk hat on his head, bowed to my father, and swayed majestically out into the street.

"My father stood in the door and watched him go.

"And when we looked, why, there were tears in his eyes.

" 'There goes my last customer,' he said, 'my very last customer.' "

Yes, these are some of the stories of the innkeeper, Paul Harel, we heard that sunny June day. And when we at last had to go I took with me something else I shall always treasure—this poem written one Christmas Eve by Paul Harel as he sat in the window of his warm, kind inn, and looked along the dark, frosty road.

POEM FOR CHRISTMAS

I wish that I had kept that inn,
That inn of old, in Bethlehem,
And Joseph had come walking in;
Dear Lord, how I'd have welcomed him!

With open arms, "Come in!" I'd say.
"What! . . . Bring her in! Do not delay."
And oh, my heart with joy would brim,
To see the smile she'd give to him.

And I'd have said to all those there,
"Depart from here! Begone elsewhere!"
Black looks, insults, I'd sweep away.
"No room for the rich in my inn today!

"Away with you! No time to lose!
I'm free! I can welcome whom I choose!"
And when they'd gone, I'd turn to him,
"Monsieur Saint Joseph, please come in!"

And then I'd bow most low and say,
"Madame Mary, come in, pray,
Draw the curtains of my best bed;
Rest, my lady, rest your dear head."

Then to my servants I would say,
"Down on our knees! Down and pray!
For oh, to me, it's wondrous clear
That Heaven itself is with us here.

"Now tiptoe round. Bake fresh white bread.
Let flowers round each dish be spread.
And I must to the stable go,
To speak to Ass, and Ox so slow.

" 'Dear creatures both!' to them I'd say,
'Rejoice with us! Look, here is hay!
Now to cellar I must away,
The shepherds must not thirsty stay.'

"Bring lights! Set lanterns everywhere,
In window, door, and on the stair.
The night is dark. This inn of mine
Like royal palace now must shine.

"Now is He born! So small, so fair,
The women weep to see Him there.
But hark! Who knocks? Led by a star
There stand three kings from lands afar.

" 'Good innkeeper, tell us plain and true,
The King of kings, is He with you?'
'Your Majesties, your search is done,
Beneath my roof is God's own Son.

" 'But Majesties, the night is cold,
Bring in your incense, myrrh, and gold.
Please . . . single file . . . the place is small,
Your robes may catch against the wall.' "

Stories of Paul Harel

And when the kings, at break of day,
I'd set, rejoicing, on their way,
Noiselessly, no need to call,
The Ass, the Ox, would leave their stall,

And we'd admire the shining gold,
The myrrh, incense, these gifts foretold.
Outside, all Bethlehem would sleep
As we our silent watch would keep.

And then, please God, we'd hear her sing,
"Jesus, my Child, my Son, my King,
Stretch out Thy hand, bless this kind inn,
And all who sleep these walls within."

And then, oh then, my heart would swell,
For I, who deserve the pangs of Hell,
I'd hear her say, "Bless him as well!
Forgive the sins of Paul Harel!"

Filling the Sandwich

Last August, B.B.C.'s "Woman's Hour" presented half a dozen broadcasters with the first and last sentence of a short story, and invited them to fill in the gap. This series was called "Filling the Sandwich". My story went like this:

ANNOUNCER: "There was an empty book of stamps, an envelope with a 1946 postmark, and a photograph which I recognised instantly . . ."

My old friend smiled as she caught my look,
"Yes, I keep them: photograph, letter and empty book;
And sometimes I think if the Lord, in His love,
Allowed us three earthly keepsakes above,
Why, there I would stand, at Heaven's door,
With these three treasures, nothing more.
And before Saint Peter could shrug his wings,
Amused to see such foolish things,
'I am Basia Balinska,' I'd boldly say
(Celestial air making me feel that way—
As if one's story must be told,
Before one went through gates of gold),
'Basia Balinska, who married so young,

Filling the Sandwich

Merry of heart and eager, and strong.
But all over Poland times already were bad,
Down French mines, they said, there was work to be had.
And we both wanted children, and to give them their
    chance,
So we sold all we had
            And went there . . . to France.

Long hours my man toiled down in that pit,
And I earned a little—I could bake, sew, and knit.
Those thrifty years brought us joy in plenty,
A son, a daughter, both nearing twenty:
Zosia, so pretty, and Josef, strong and tall,
And we, who'd come there with nothing at all,
We bought our own house, pear-tree on wall.
And there I'd work and sing the live-long day,
'Those Poles! They don't worry!' our neighbours would say.
They were right. We asked nothing more.
This was our home.
            Why think then of war!

Those bombs!
        They killed my son, my man.
        And there we ran,
My girl and I, in that frenzied throng,
That fled the roads of France along.
Machine-gunned; bombed; no one to explain.
'Avion!' we'd cry, and crouch in ditches again.
A truck, packed with school-girls, came crawling through
    smoke,
The nun, driving it, leaned out and spoke:

Filling the Sandwich

She could take one more.
        So I cried, 'Up you go!
Don't cry, little silly! We'll meet in Bordeaux!'

And there I stood smiling, my poor heart like lead,
As that truckload of youth went plunging ahead.

To that sight I clung for six bitter years,
Stifling all doubts, all desperate fears;
For ask where I might, none seemed to know
If that nun and her truck ever came to Bordeaux.
But ships from Bordeaux fled to England, they said.
So I fiercely hoped on. Would not think her dead.

As soon as it ended I found a way,
I went to England; and day after day,
When I wasn't working, long hours I'd spend
In refugee centres; and, dear Lord, the letters I'd send!
French, Polish, British; they were all very kind,
But not a trace of my Zosia, not a trace could they find.

And now a strange numbness began to creep
Into my heart as I tried to sleep,
How would I live, of all hope bereft?
How would I live—with no one left?

And I'd get up and write all over again,
In Polish, in French, I'd try to explain,
But back came that terrible: 'Madame, nous regrettons . . .'
Regrets . . . regrets . . . always 'nous regrettons . . .'

At last, with my weary self I made a pact,
One more book of stamps; then I'd face the bitter fact.

Filling the Sandwich

I would admit it; bow my stubborn old head.
I was alone. My Zosia was dead.

Nineteen forty-six crawled to its desolate close,
Christmas Eve, midnight, was the hour I chose:
Renounce vain hope, vain search forsake,
And courage beg, for Christ's sweet sake.

I came down that morning, my heart cold as stone,
From the silent room where I lived alone.
I crossed myself; I could hardly see,
My old eyes, I said, were mocking me,
But there it still shone—from America, addressed plain to
    me.
Zosia . . . my Zosia . . . was writing to me!

'Mama, Mamusia, I am safe, happy, well,
But everything, all that happened, next time I will tell.
Today I'm too happy; I keep singing instead,
That letter was wrong! My mother's not dead!
And my husband is laughing, "Send her this photo as well!
Tell her all kids need a granny; now everything's swell!"'

And there, in my photo, she smiles up at me,
Three little ones, one each side, and one upon her knee,
And there stands her husband, as proud as can be.
Dear Lord, how lovely all five look to me!

That Christmas Eve I heard them sing,
'Glory to our new-born King!'
And I, who thought to be kneeling there,
Lost in loneliness and cold despair,

Filling the Sandwich

I sang 'Gloria!', my heart aglow.
The clock could strike, but I would know,
I, who had thought myself bereft,
When midnight came . . .
            'There were SIX OF US left!'"

Carol of Saint Basil

━━━━━━━━━━━━━━━━━━━━━━━━

Some time ago I came across an old book called *Carols from Many Lands*.

Among them was one that went:

Begins the day,
Begins the year,
January again is here,
See from Caesarea town
Good Saint Basil coming down.

And the footnote said: "This ancient carol is sung by *Greek* children on New Year's Eve."

Now this interested me, especially when I found out that on New Year's Eve children all over Greece go from door to door, still singing this carol. And to help out the singing they bang away on anything that makes a melodious clang; and if one of them has a mouth-organ, well, so much the better. Then one of them also carries a large tin decorated with bright paper flowers—for appreciative offerings, of course; money, sweets or fruit.

But when I began to ask why they sang a New Year carol about Saint Basil coming down from Caesarea town nobody knew. Just an old Greek custom, I was told.

The story-teller in me wasn't satisfied with *that*, for by now I had looked up Caesarea, and it is perched high in the foothills of a district called Cappadocia— in *Turkey*.

As for Saint Basil, he turned out to be a learned and scholarly monk who lived *sixteen hundred years ago*!

Yet here were the children of Greece still singing of him as if it were yesterday.

Must be a story—a *reason* for all this—somewhere. But look where I might, I couldn't find one, till one day in the British Museum Library I blew the dust from a book written well over a hundred years ago by a Frenchman who had wandered round the mountain villages of Cappadocia jotting down the stories they told there of a winter's evening around the stove.

Suddenly, if I hadn't been in that solemn library, I'd have shouted for joy! For there in those musty yellow pages shone the story I was seeking, the tale behind the Carol of Saint Basil.

"Saint Basil was born in these parts but he did what all young noblemen did in those days—he crossed the sea to study in the city of Athens in Greece. In those days, Turkey and Greece were all part of one big empire. And soon all Athens was singing his praises, for Basil not only learned to discourse of learned things, but he spoke with so golden a tongue that even the poor and simple understood him.

"Basil will make a famous lawyer, they said. Or a statesman. Or an orator.

"Great was their surprise when they heard that Basil had no ambition whatever, save to work for God in his native land.

" 'You'll be wasted there!' they said.

"But Basil followed his heart, and came back to his lands near Caesarea. And with him came other men who thought as he did. Together they ploughed the fields, and planted corn, and olive groves, and vineyards.

"This done, they built a hospital for the sick and old, and an orphanage for the children nobody wanted; and kindest of all, high in the pines, they built a home for *lepers*—with a workshop; for Basil knew that each of us needs to feel he is at least useful.

"And so the quiet years went by; the cornfields rippled in the sun, the olive trees burst into tiny scented flowers, and the vines grew thick and strong on the mountainside. And from dawn to dusk Basil and his monks toiled away, caring nothing for themselves, only for others.

"One afternoon a messenger came panting down from Caesarea. A great army was now resting in the meadowland outside the gate, and it was their new emperor, yes, Julian himself, who was leading that army to wage war on Persia.

" 'Basil,' said the messenger, 'the emperor bids me remind you that you were once students together in Athens. He says you are to come and eat with him, and

that he regrets the necessity but he must ask you to
provide the food.'

"Basil straightway sent the emperor all the food they
then had—bread, cheese, and radishes—and promised
he would come the moment he could be spared. There
were many sick in the hospital that year.

"Now the Emperor Julian had cast off Christ, calling him 'the pale Galilean', and he now worshipped
the pagan gods of old. So he had no patience whatever
with monks who wasted their time on the weak of this
world. And he sent soldiers to bring Basil, by force
if necessary.

"By this time, of course, all the people had crowded
out from Caesarea; and they watched with dismay as
their emperor threw the bread, cheese, and radishes in
Basil's face, shouting that he had no stomach for this
monkish joke. Food fit for an emperor, was it! Well,
he would crack joke against joke. And he stooped and
plucked a handful of grass, and thrust it into Basil's
face. 'Take it,' he bellowed. 'Stuff yourself with that!'

"But on seeing this the people burst into cheers.
'Oh, most noble Julian!' they shouted. 'Oh, most
generous emperor!'

" 'Now the gods grant me patience!' stormed Julian.
'Are you all lunatics here?'

"Basil said no, and explained that the vast meadow
on which they stood was crown land. It passed from
one emperor to another. No man might drive his flocks
to graze there on pain of death. Only the horses for
Julian's imperial army could graze there. But it was

Carol of Saint Basil

an ancient law in Cappadocia that if a man plucked grass from his meadow and publicly offered it to another man, then that was a sign, a solemn pledge that he gave him the right to graze his flocks there for evermore.

"And as Basil and his monks shared all they had, the people knew that from now on they, too, would be able to drive their flocks to graze on this rich meadowland.

"Julian, white with rage, said in that case he must pile gratitude on gratitude. He would present these cheering lunatics with still more land on which to turn their beasts.

"And he swore by all his pagan gods, by Castor and Polydeuces, that when he returned from his war on Persia he would lay low the hospital, the orphanage, all Basil's monkish buildings, every one. And then he would level the town of Caesarea with the ground. Yes, he would give them *space* on which to graze their flocks!

"And, still storming, he ordered the trumpets to sound, and rode forth at the head of his army.

"The people of Caesarea watched him go, hearts heavy as lead within them.

"But the frightened children came crowding about Basil, and to calm them he led them to a quiet place where a brave soldier of old, called Mercurius, lay buried. There was a stone figure of him there, dressed in armour, lying flat on his back, on the top of his tomb. And Basil told the children how Mercurius had been a giant of a man and a very fine soldier, and when threatened with torture he had refused to cast off Christ, and went most bravely to his death, thus proving again that 'perfect love casteth out fear'. And as the children listened to the golden voice of Basil, they looked at the quiet stone face of Mercurius. And their fear fell from them and presently they went quietly home to their beds.

"Now explain this if you can, but they say that very night as the Emperor Julian lay on his bed a giant of a soldier came striding into his tent. And he greeted the emperor, saying he was Mercurius, Captain of the Light Infantry.

"Julian sharply said the Light Infantry had not worn that type of iron breast-plate these fifty years.

"Oh, longer than that, said Mercurius. For he died in the year of grace 260, and it was now 382. So this breast-plate of his was well over a hundred years old.

"It was then that Julian knew he was dreaming. And he laughed to himself when he heard Mercurius warn him to forget his cruel threats against the monk Basil and the town of Caesarea. 'Otherwise,' said Mercurius, 'I shall feel obliged to lend the Persians a hand!'

"The emperor laughed again. Here was a merry dream! Mercurius, a century dead, threatening to lead the Persian Light Infantry against him, a living emperor!

"And he laughed so loud that he woke himself up. And found himself alone in his tent. And suddenly very cold. And with no mind to laugh.

"As for the people of Caesarea, they made one anxious plan after another to offer rich gifts to Julian

153

when he came back, and so turn away his anger. And the days dragged into weeks, and the weeks into months, and on the last day of the year a messenger on a sweating horse came galloping through their gate . . . with news at last from the Persian front.

"The emperor was dead. Slain in battle. The Persians had outwitted him from the start. If he pursued them, they led him into cunning ambush. If he stood his ground, they refused to join battle, but sent great stones volleying down the mountainside to keep him well on the jump. And day by day the emperor grew more distraught. He would utter strange words, saying a wily old fox of a veteran called Mercurius had thrown in his lot with the Persians. And when he lay dying of a Persian lance he had cried:

" 'My gods are shattered. The pale Galilean has triumphed. Go, tell the monk Basil of Caesarea!'

"When they heard this, the children looked at each other. Here was something to remember, to pass on to other children.

"And that New Year's Eve as Basil came through the Gate of Caesarea his face shone. For there stood all the children, and one big lad cried:

" 'Now, shall we start?'

"And another shouted:

" 'Yes, off we go!'

"And all the children struck up their music whilst the big boys sang a song to Saint Basil—just as they do to this very day."

I am an Investigator

I'd never realised that I *was* an investigator until the other day when somebody called me one. And when I'd got over the surprise of being considered something so high-sounding I was even more gratified to look myself up in the dictionary and discover I really was one—of a sort.

Investigate: to search into, to inquire into with care.

Now I'll admit I cannot endure inquiring with care into everything—where the money goes, for instance, or how my sewing-machine works. I let that sort of thing go on baffling me. But if something inside begins to mutter, "There's a story somewhere here!", then off I go, searching and inquiring, the most ardent of investigators.

Last June, for instance, my husband and I spent ten days in a little seaside place called Carnac-Plage on the south coast of Brittany. It's just down the road from the village of Carnac, and a leaflet from the French Railways promised us that there were pine trees there, and that it was quiet, sunny, and very reasonable. And if we felt so inclined, close-by there were mega-lithic monuments—prehistoric stones to you and me.

But I wasn't interested in any monuments, prehistoric or otherwise—after all, I'd seen Stonehenge. All I wanted to do was sit and stare—in a comfortable chair too—under those pine trees.

Well, Carnac-Plage turned out all we'd hoped it would be—silver sands, blue sea, white villas set among tall pine trees, and, being out of season, next to nothing else to stare at.

Or so I thought—till one morning I noticed that we were walking along a quiet road called Avenue James Miln.

Now what was a road in a small French seaside village doing with a name like that?

"Meeln?" said the girl who brought us our coffee. "Ah yes, Meeln of course! Then Madame hasn't been there yet?"

I said no, I hadn't. And what was it?

And she said the museum of course, up at Carnac, the Museum James Meeln. And off she flew to have a few words with the postman.

Now, what was a village the size of Carnac doing with a museum, a museum called "Musée James Miln"?

No, there was nothing for it but to drink up our coffee and go and find out.

A quarter of an hour later I was having a wonderful conversation with an old lady I'd met outside the church. I'd asked her the way to the museum, and she said she'd take us there. In fact she *insisted* on taking us there. She said she was only a little girl at the time but she distinctly remembered seeing Monsieur Meeln, the good man, before he went back to Scotland. Oh yes, he'd come from Scotland, to look at the menhirs, the old stones; some people called them the Soldiers of Saint Cornély, but one couldn't swallow everything, could one?

And I said no, indeed, and who was Saint Cornély? And she said his statue was in the church, a very nice gilt one, and I really ought to go and pay him a little visit. But to come back to Monsieur Meeln, the good man. Now he had come to Carnac for a week or so, and he had stayed seven years. Seven years! That would show me, hein? And it was a thousand pities the poor man ever went back to this Scotland of his, because he straightway caught a fever there and died, to the great grief of all Carnac, the good clever man!

But not before he had founded his museum, of course! And what was in it? Why, the things he'd dug up. And here was the museum, so we could see them for ourselves. And au-revoir and a happy holiday to us both. And she stood and saw us safely inside.

It was a strange little museum, almost rustic, and yet the kind of place where you find yourself talking in whispers. For there, in the glass-cases, lay the weapons, the tools, the cooking-pots, the necklaces, the bangles, the lucky charms of men, women and children of well over four thousand years ago. I remember there was one skeleton of a young mother lying close to her baby. And somehow it wasn't gruesome. It was touching.

157

I am an Investigator

And everything, just as it was arranged, seventy long years ago, by a man from Scotland, called James Miln.

Suddenly it swept over me again. Here, oh, here was a story, calling, imploring to be found and told.

But here also was my husband, patient but ravenous. So we went back to our little hotel for a meal.

That afternoon we set off to see the stones. I'll never forget it. Behind us we left Carnac-Plage, gay, friendly, modern. And presently we turned a corner, and there, on either side of the road, stretched a wild moor, broken here and there by sombre groups of dark pine trees.

And there they were, those strange grey stones, set up by men four thousand years ago, some no bigger than a milestone, some as tall as a house. We counted eleven lines of them, eleven straight lines, looking for all the world like a grotesque army on the march.

We walked alongside, through the heather, the gorse, and the tall purple orchids, through a dark little wood of pines, and out and across the moor again till we came to a quiet lake. And right through that lake went those stones—we could see their heads sticking up above the water—and over there, on the other side, off they went again, row upon row, on and on, through the bracken, the blackberry bushes and the ragged sweet camomile.

But we sat down on a low stone wall for a rest. Behind us a great field of corn shone in the sun.

What manner of men were these who set up these

stones? And why? And why did some people call them the Soldiers of Saint Cornély?

Then, suddenly, it was evening. And behind every grey stone slanted a purple shadow. And I can't explain it, but now there was a stern grandeur, a solemnity about those stones; it was almost as if we were sitting in some vast, ancient cathedral. And in a queer, groping way I knew what had kept James Miln seven years at Carnac. He, too, had felt there was a story here. He, too, was an investigator.

The next morning I called on Saint Cornély in Carnac Church. I found him in a glass case that looked remarkably like a gaudy doll's-house. But the saint himself was very majestic. He wore a triple crown— this shows he was a Pope—and just below his handsome beard was a round window, for all the world like a porthole in his chest. A loving little angel leaned on each shoulder, and there below the saint was a marble table with cows painted on it. Yes, cows. Two of them, one each side of a pool of blue painted water.

A saint—with a porthole in his chest—and cows— and soldiers.

So I spoke to a little nun kneeling by my side. And she said Saint Cornély was the patron saint of all animals with horns, but especially perhaps cows and oxen. And what a pity it was I couldn't stay till September when the people from miles around flocked into Carnac with their cattle. "Such a fine procession," she said, "all round the village, and then Monsieur le Curé comes out and blesses them."

I am an Investigator

And, said the little nun, there were old people who declared that if these good beasts were not treated to this pilgrimage, why, they'd find their way to Carnac alone. As for the window in the chest of the saint, that of course was to show the relic inside, undoubtedly a most ancient relic, since Saint Cornély lived in the time of the Romans.

Then the bell began to ring the Angelus, so I said "Merci, ma sœur", and she said not at all, it was always a pleasure to talk about their good saint.

But as I walked out into the sunshine there was the investigator in me, muttering away, "Yes, but what about the Soldiers of Saint Cornély? What about *them*?"

And, well, that afternoon, there we were again, walking alongside those stones. But this time we stepped it out, and presently we came to a wild desolate stretch where the stones suddenly grew enormous. And there, racing towards us, came a band of six or seven children, shrieking "A moi! A moi!"—"My turn! My turn!"

And the first to reach us panted: "Voulez-vous que je vous récite la Légende des Menhirs?" "Would you like me to recite the Legend of the Menhirs?"

"Combien?" asked my cautious husband. "How much?"

The boy gave him a winning smile. "Oh, what Monsieur pleases. A hundred francs, yes?"

"A hundred francs, NO!" I said. "Tell me, are you then a band of young brigands?"

"Ah no, madame," he assured me. "I thought Monsieur was perhaps American!"

"Well, he isn't!" I said. "Now let's have the real price."

So we settled on fifty francs, inclusive, and all seven of them took a deep breath and began to chant:

"Ces pierres alignées sont des soldats transformés en pierre par Monsieur Saint Cornély . . ."

"Listen," I said. "I'd prefer just *one* of you to tell it, and not like that, but in your own words."

"Very well, madame," they said, and nudged a dark-eyed boy in a black overall.

And he began:

"Monsieur Saint Cornély was the Pope in Rome, madame. And he wanted to teach everybody else about the good God. So he set off in a cart drawn by two oxen. But when Caesar heard about it—he was a pagan, madame—he was furious and sent a great army to track down Monsieur Saint Cornély and kill him.

"So Monsieur Saint Cornély had to travel on and on. When he came to this place he was very tired, and he said, 'I will stay here and build a church at Carnac.'

"But then he heard them again, tramp-tramp-tramp. The Roman soldiers, madame. 'Ah no!' said Monsieur Saint Cornély, and he hid inside the ear of one of his oxen. Yes, madame, that's what the legend says, he hid inside its ear. And the Roman soldiers went marching by, hundreds of them. And Monsieur Saint Cornély said, 'Ah no! I've had enough of this!' So

L 161

he changed all the soldiers into stones. These stones, madame. That's why they are called the Soldiers of Saint Cornély.

"But they're not all here, madame. Some of them are missing, because people used to take them to patch their walls. But they can't do it now because they all belong to the Government."

"And a good thing, too!" I said. "The very idea! Taking a Roman soldier to patch a wall! Enough to make Caesar turn in his grave!"

"Yes, madame," he said. "Would you like to buy some postcards?"

So we paid up, and bought some postcards, and off they tore to greet a whole coach-load of sightseers, chanting: "Voulez-vous que je vous récite la Légende des Menhirs ?"

"Okay!" came a voice from the coach. And yes, these *were* Americans!

And we walked on, and my husband said, "You know, we really ought to have looked this place up in a good guide-book."

"What!" I said. "And miss all these surprises!"

I ask you, what a thing to say to an investigator!

Reflections on Pictures

I went to the Exhibition at the Royal Academy the other day. Not that I know the first thing about art. I don't. I just enjoy looking at pictures—even the very modern sort that makes me wonder which of us is a shade peculiar—me or the artist.

For instance, in this year's Exhibition there's a picture of a group of people who've just had a dip—in a nearby river, I presume—as they are now drying off in a meadow, hemmed in on all sides by outsizes in cows. Not my idea of comfort. But that's not what intrigued me. It was the way I simply couldn't sort out their faces. From the neck up they melted, as you might say, into the landscape and the cows. Even so, that's not why I stood so long before this picture. No, it set me thinking about a rag picture-book I once bought for my daughter. She was about a year old at the time, I suppose, for she still expressed her feelings not in words but in yells and gurgles. And she fairly doted on this picture-book—all except page six. When we came to this she always gave a piercing shriek and hastily turned over to blot out the awful sight, whatever it was. I couldn't make it out. It was such a pleasant homely picture—a dear little girl modestly stepping into a nice warm bath. Nothing in the least frightening. Nice little face with all the usual features, two arms, two legs, one foot on the mat, the other in the water. IN THE WATER . . . NOT VISIBLE! Perhaps that was it. So I took pen and ink and somehow managed to sketch in the submerged foot.

And the following evening, when we came to page six, there was a deep, deep sigh, followed by joyous gurgles. The little girl had found her foot. All was well.

Mind you, I'm not suggesting that I could improve upon that picture in the Academy by sketching in a few comfortable faces. Heavens, no! I can almost hear the artist tartly telling me that it's crystal clear that I'm still in my infancy too, so far as art is concerned—hankering after faces like that.

And maybe I am, for when I look back on all the pictures I've seen in my time I have to admit that the ones I remember best are NOT the ones I *ought* to remember —that is, if I had twopennyworth of the real artist in me.

I had the luck to be born in Holland, for instance, and many, many a time have I been marched in to see the great works of art in Amsterdam and The Hague. And do I now remember standing there lost in admiration before "The Night Watch" or some such master-piece? No, I don't. But I do most clearly and fondly recall two masterpieces on my Dutch grandmother's parlour walls. Problem pictures they were. Perhaps you remember them too. Every picture told a story. And the fashion in Holland in those days was for the tragic problem—the deeper the gloom, the better the picture. And my Dutch grandmother had a choice pair.

The one over the piano showed a magnificent flight of marble steps in some wondrous, southern garden. Down these gleaming steps came a pair of fond lovers, she, blonde and lovely in a pale-blue satin gown with a long flowing train sweeping the marble steps behind her; he, just wonderful in a white and scarlet uniform all laced with gold, and carrying his shining brass helmet under his arm. Oh, a most romantic couple! But wait, who is this who lurks behind the palms at the foot of the marble steps? It is a scowling brunette, in rich green silk. One hand clutches a letter, the other a sinister black bottle, a bottle that undoubtedly holds something nasty. Is she about to drink its dreadful contents or hurl it at the loving pair?

Well, your guess is as good as mine.

And did this picture have a most shocking effect on our young and innocent minds? Not on your life! We adored it. We called the blonde Lily, the brunette Rosie, and the dashing hussar Gussie. And our favourite theory was that the moment Lily and Gussie reached the bottom of the marble stairs, out would dash Rosie, saying, "Can I interest you in our patent stain-remover? Guaranteed to remove all spots, including ink and mildew. Only one guilder the bottle!"

And we regarded the companion picture—the one that hung over the what-not—with even more affectionate levity.

This one showed a roaring river, simply rampaging

through a bleak and wintry landscape. And standing on its very brink were a plump gentleman and an even plumper lady; he very smart in tight, striped grey trousers, black morning coat, tall silk hat and a most expensive diamond tie-pin; she, regal in purple velvet, with one of those fine massive busts all in one piece, with a gold watch pinned on it.

And well may you ask what they were doing there, on the river bank, on so cold a winter's day. I'll tell you. They were standing face to face, and they were firmly lashed together with a length of strong rope!

Were they about to leap into the raging river? And if so, why?

All I know is that we worked out the very neatest solution to the problem.

They were just waiting for a crowd to gather. And when a satisfactory number had assembled, the gentleman would invite some lucky spectator to give them a hearty shove. In they would topple with an almighty splash. And swim under water whilst the gentleman swiftly undid the rope. Then, to loud applause, they would reappear, swim back to the shore, and briskly proceed to hand round the tall silk hat, into which the cheering crowd would toss every coin they had in their pockets.

Ah me, there are no such pictures nowadays. But one never knows. Already bright young things are eagerly buying up what they are pleased to call "Victoriana". So who knows? Maybe my grandmother's prize pair of pictures will again hang in pride of place— on her great-great-grandson's walls.

One Silent Night

Christmas Eve, 1818.

Down a frozen track in the Austrian Alps hurried a young priest on his way back to his church in the mountain village of Hallein. Overhead the moon shone in the cold clear sky, and the snow sparkled blue-white on the mountainside, the forests, the sloping roofs of Hallein in the valley below. A lovely night.

But Father Mohr was thinking of an even lovelier sight. That afternoon a woman had come knocking at his door. She said a child had been born to the wife of the charcoal-burner; yes, the young couple who lived in the lonely hut on the edge of the forest high above the village. Would Father Mohr please go there and baptise the baby?

So Father Mohr had closed his Bible, pushed back his half-finished sermon, and climbed up to that poor little hut. And now, as he hurried back through all the crisp loveliness of that frosty night, he still saw the face of the young mother as she smiled down on her sleeping child. So must Mary have smiled on our Little Lord. Now if he could only write a sermon for Christmas

One Silent Night

Day, a sermon that would express all the tenderness, the quiet joy, the holiness of that scene . . .

If only it wasn't so late! As it was, he would only be just in time for Midnight Mass.

Very well, he would sit up, all night if necessary, for he *must* set down all he felt in his heart.

So that moonlit night, when all his parishioners had gone home to their beds, Father Mohr sat on at his desk, trying to write his Christmas sermon. But the words that came to him refused to be pinned down into neat, clerical sentences, but sang to him like all the bells of Heaven, and refused to be silenced. And when Christmas morning broke, there on his desk lay no sermon but a poem.

A poem . . .! Now what was he to do for a sermon? As he stared at it, his friend, Franz Gruber, came hurrying in. Now Franz was not only the village schoolmaster, he also played the organ in the church. And Father Mohr gave one look at his face and said, "In trouble, Franz?"

"Trouble!" groaned Franz Gruber. "Those mice have been at it again!"

"Not the new hymn-books!" asked Father Mohr.

"Worse! Far worse! The organ this time! They must have been gnawing away inside all night! I can't get a note out of her! No music . . . and on Christmas Day!"

"Franz," said Father Mohr, and held out his poem, "set this to music; oh, something quite simple that you can play on your guitar, and let's sing it at Mass this morning, you and I."

One Silent Night

"Be sensible, Father," urged Franz. "Compose a melody in so short a time!"

"Franz," said Father Mohr, "please look at it. I don't know how I know it, but I *know* you can do it!"

He was right. Just as the words had come singing to him, so the melody they made sang clear and sweet to Franz Gruber. And that Christmas morning, in the village church of Hallein, Father Mohr stood by his friend as he played his guitar, and they both sang their new Christmas carol. And not a soul missed the organ, but sat caught up in wonder. So must the angels, the shepherds have sung . . . over there in Bethlehem. . . .

As soon as they could afford it the people of Hallein sent for old Karl Mauracher, who lived in a neighbouring village. Karl was an organ-builder and he could be trusted to mend their organ with skill and economy. And when he had repaired all the damage done by the hungry mice he turned to Franz Gruber.

"Try it," he said. "I think everything is all right now."

So Franz sat down and tried the pedals and notes, and presently, why, there he was playing and singing the new carol, the one they had sung on Christmas Day.

"But that is beautiful! Beautiful!" said old Karl Mauracher.

"I'll write it down for you," said Franz, very pleased.

"No, no, just play it again. I shall remember it."

So Franz Gruber played it again, and old Karl went home with still another lovely song safe in his head.

And soon, every child in *his* valley too knew the new carol, and with the swift instinct of children they gave it the perfect name. They called it the "Song from Heaven".

Now one of Karl's neighbours was a glovemaker called Strausser. He had four children: Caroline, Joseph, Andreas, and little Amalie. And all the winter long as they helped Father and Mother stitch the soft chamois-leather gloves, or sew on the buttons, the four children loved to sing. "Those Straussers," said the neighbours, "those Straussers sing like nightingales."

When spring came the Straussers would pack up all their gloves and set out for the Annual Fair in the great city of Leipzig. There, they would rig up a stall, and carefully arrange their beautiful gloves. And soon they would all be hard at it, trying them on, and selling them to the passers-by. But when business was slack the children did just what they did at home. They sang. And one day they looked up to see an elderly gentleman standing there, listening to them.

"I see you understand music," he said. "Would you like tickets for the grand concert this evening at the Guildhall?"

So that evening, in the plush and splendour of the Guildhall, there sat our four children, very over-awed, watching the distinguished audience take up their seats. Oh, a most distinguished audience; the King and Queen of Saxony, and all their high-born retinue, ladies in silks and satins, and gentlemen in frock-coats, carrying their tall, silk hats.

But when the concert began they forgot all this. Music! Such music! Ach, such music!

Then they sat up with a start. Up there, on the platform, bowing to the audience, was the elderly gentleman, the one who had given them their tickets. And what was that he was saying? He was saying that there were four children in the audience who had the finest voices he had ever heard, and he was now going to invite them to come up on the platform and sing to their gracious Majesties.

"He's waving to us!" whispered Andreas.

"We can't! Not here, before all these people!"

"But they're waiting, clapping . . . for us!"

And one simply cannot keep a king and queen waiting, so the four children, hearts thumping, cheeks burning, stumbled up on the platform.

"Shut your eyes," ordered sensible Caroline. "Pretend we're home."

So they all shut their eyes and sang. And the first song they sang was the one they loved the best, the song old Karl Mauracher had taught them—the "Song from Heaven".

Then they sang another song. On and on they sang, all the lovely old Tyrolean airs. And when they had finished they sang it again, their favourite, their beloved "Song from Heaven".

For a moment there was silence, a lovely silence, far more moving than all the applause that then tore up to the roof. And presently the four bewildered children found themselves in the royal box, bowing and

171

curtseying to their Majesties, the King and Queen of Saxony.

"That Christmas song," asked the Queen. "Where did you learn it?"

"From Karl Mauracher, Your Majesty. He heard it played by Franz Gruben over in Hallein, and it was Father Mohr who wrote the words."

"Next Christmas," said the Queen, "we will send for you. And you shall sing it to our children."

The Queen, as good queens do, kept her promise. The following Christmas Eve the four Strausser children sang Father Mohr's carol to the royal children and all the court of Saxony.

And it was as if the carol they sang spread its gentle wings and went singing, on and on, all over Europe, and then across the seven seas, straight into every heart. "Silent night, holy night," sang the children, just as they do to this very day.

Meek Wives

I don't suppose we women have ever come in for more flattering attention than we get lavished on us nowadays. Kind gentlemen of all parties say and write the very nicest things about us; gallant house-wives, the backbone of the nation—that's us, nowadays.

In the days of yore, now, gentlemen with gold watch-chains slung across their middles used to crack playful jokes about "Woman, man's greatest blessing, and his greatest plague". By the way, it was Euripides of Ancient Greece who thought of that one; but you know men—clothes, pipes, jokes, the older they are, the better they like them.

But today, it would appear, we are everybody's greatest blessing.

Now I quite fancy myself as a blessing. So why don't I burst into a loud hear-hear when I listen to these songs of praise? Why do I catch myself muttering, "Oh, come off it!" when the music in our honour swells oh, so complimentary?

Well, what really goes on in this brave new world of ours? Let's start with something forever with us— the washing-up. Most husbands nowadays lend a hand

with that. But what does every man of them say as
he swaggers off, leaving *us* to tackle the meat tin, mop
up the floor and scour the greasy sink? I needn't tell
you. You'll have heard it. "There! I've washed up for
you." Yes, they always wash-up for *us*—as if we, and
we alone, had used all those knives, forks, spoons and
plates, not to mention the saucepans that ten to one
they've left high, dry and dirty on the stove.

Then there's the well-meaning husband who solemnly
broadcasts that he himself favours the idea that mothers
should have a night out occasionally.

Bless his simple heart, we've favoured that little
notion for centuries. Way back in Ancient Greece a
merry gentleman called Aristophanes wrote a comedy
in which a chorus of ladies tripped out and demanded:

> *Pray why do you men like us always to be at home*
> *Ready to smile and to greet you,*
> *Why are you injured and hard-done-by*
> *If your wife isn't there to meet you?*

And that was well over two thousand years ago. Still,
it's nice to think we're gradually getting the idea over,
isn't it?

I think you'll be interested to hear that same lady-
like chorus then heaved a sigh and went on to recite:

> *And, oh, how well we know the jokes*
> *The jokes men love to make.*

And so we do. Week in, week out, we listen to them.
But there is one stock joke that I do take exception

to, because it's been dead so long that it ought to have been buried long ago—the mother-in-law joke.

Now I'm nobody's mother-in-law, yet, but I think it's about time somebody sang the sober praises of the hundreds of thousands of mothers-in-law who never appear in the headlines, never draw attention to themselves in any way. They are the everyday sort. They run their own homes, and they can also be relied upon to look after their grandchildren by the hour, the day, and sometimes for weeks on end. And if this sort of mother-in-law comes to stay, she arrives with her pinafore, and starts rolling her sleeves up at the garden gate, for there's either sickness in the house or else there's going to be a new baby any minute now. And as she gets down to her overtime, does anybody ever sing her praises on the air? No, not even a kindly joke— just the same dreary old mixture. Why don't these jesters step out of their cloud-cuckoo world and have a look at us ordinary women?

And at this point I can hear them saying, "The trouble with you women is that you've not got a sense of humour." And if we say, "Really? What makes you think that?" they say, "Well—just look at your hats."

Okay, let's look at *their* hats!

Have you ever seen anything quite so dreary as a window full of gents' hats? "So dull, so dead in look, so woebegone"—Shakespeare's words, not mine. And have you ever considered that other dusty futility— the turn-ups of trousers? Do you remember how during the war, when we were all out to save time and material, there was a regulation that no trousers were to have turn-ups? And what happened? The men *outside* the Government got at the men *inside* the Government. And back came the turn-ups as natty as ever. And all the while we meek women were gnashing our teeth at our comic corsets and peculiar stockings and other afflictions—but did anyone heed *us*? Oh no, they all thought it rather funny—especially the corsets. And, as you well know, there's nothing funny about a corset. On the contrary, a good corset is a very real and urgent necessity for countless women. But turn-ups now! Can't you imagine the merry quips we'd hear if we women always bought skirts two inches too long, just so that we could turn them up and make a nice dust-collector all round the hem?

And talking about jokes, do you know what I'd dearly love to write? A satirical poem—or, if I couldn't rise to that, a devastating article all about that MAN'S GAME—CRICKET. Oh, how I'd enjoy taking a tilt at twenty-two gentlemen, in virgin white, smacking a little ball all over the place, and millions of other gentlemen listening in to the results in reverential silence. Joke! Why, to me, that masculine game is downright hilarious. But, of course, most cricketers' wives and mothers are kept far too busy washing and ironing all their nice white rig-outs to see the funny side of it. I'll never forget the day I gave a dirty look at a pile on my kitchen floor and said, "In Heaven's name, why white? It's only a game . . . what's wrong with a serviceable grey?"

Meek Wives

"Grey!" hooted my son. "That just shows you're only half British!" (The other half of me is sensible Dutch!) No true British wife and mother, it seems, would ever joke about cricket—at least not the way I do. It is NOT cricket. And they are NOT amused.

And I'll tell you something else that makes me guffaw very loud and vulgar: the advertisements in any newspaper, especially about Christmas-time. What do we get from these gentlemen who frame the advertisements to captivate the fancy of other men? "Buy her a lovely mangle for Christmas and see her face light up! Give her a set of our beautiful saucepans and watch her smile!"

Smile! We could laugh our heads off—if we weren't so kind, and grateful for any little attention. But tell me, have you ever spotted an advertisement that ran: "Buy him a set of brushes this Christmas to sweep the chimney for Santa Claus"? No, of course you haven't. Neither have I.

No, the more I reflect on all this—and much besides—the more I am driven to conclude that the remarkable thing about us gallant housewives—the backbone of the nation, etc., etc.—is not the way we still go on putting our gallant backs into all the jobs nobody else wants to do—it is our amazing patience. Hang it all, we've been listening to the same jokes about ourselves for centuries. Is that a record, or is it not? And if it is, why, oh why won't they put another nickel in, or, better still, why not switch the darn thing off. The backbone of this nation has had about enough of it.

Gentlemen, we may seem meek, but we are NOT amused.

Young Pierre Scrooge

I was twenty, and spending the winter with a large and lively family in France. The village church badly needed a new harmonium, and the family felt that with an English Miss right there on the spot to direct, a "Grande Fête de Noël Charles Dickens" was absolutely indicated to swell the harmonium-fund.

Monsieur le Curé not only enthusiastically agreed, he also ordered the rapturous Catechism Class to place themselves entirely at my service. And for three crowded December weeks we slaved on our secret programme—behind the locked doors of the roomy Salle de Ping-Pong of the Restaurant Saint Isidore kindly put at our disposal by Madame La Patronne. We also spent one long afternoon in the forest and tramped back laden with ivy, holly, and a fine young fir tree, and singing "Tipperary" at the tops of our voices.

On Christmas afternoon parents and friends crowded into the Restaurant Saint Isidore and eagerly bought pink programmes that promised them a veritable Feast of British Christmas Music, Dances, Games, Gifts and Traditional Refreshment.

178

And though I say so myself, we did them proud.

The "Salle de Ping-Pong", for instance, was transformed. Trails of ivy, branches of holly, gay paper chains, and a great bunch of mistletoe dangled from the beams overhead. Next to the piano, kindly lent to us by the schoolmistress, towered our Christmas tree, little gifts in coloured wrappings hanging on every branch. And the Catechism Class, hopping with excitement, chorused "Merry Chreestmas" to all newcomers, and then fairly swept them into the chairs lined up against the walls.

The Feast began with cups of tea all round, served as in Britain with milk and sugar. In those days rural France had no opinion whatever of tea, save as a medicinal draught, but they drank it up with determined politeness.

However, they swiftly cheered up again when Mademoiselle Fortier sat down to her piano, and twelve boys and girls took up their positions in two lines, and danced a rousing Sir Roger de Coverley.

Then with much Gallic uproar four tables from the restaurant were pushed together, and four of the older boys who went to the local Lycée gave us a scene, in English, from *The Christmas Carol*, written, as Monsieur le Curé announced, by the great Charles himself.

And when young Pierre Scrooge, eyes flashing, arms waving, declared that the idiot who went about with "Merry Chreestmas" on his lips should be buried "in ees own pouding with a stake of 'olly tro ees eart",

179

he struck so magnificent an attitude that everybody rose to their feet and cheered and cheered.

We then cheered in Father Christmas (our genial doctor), and he proceeded to distribute the presents from the tree with little jokes in what we all told each other was a priceless British accent—Maurice Chevalier in reverse as it were, especially when he claimed his traditional British right to kiss all the grannies under the mistletoe.

Then, to loud chords on the piano, we carried in a Christmas pudding, a truly British one. I made it, so I know. But, alas, we couldn't turn it out of its large basin because I had blithely taken "quarter of a pint of milk to mix" to be the same as a quarter of a litre. So we ladled it out into saucers, and they tackled it with spoons.

After this the children gathered round the Christmas tree and sang carols—in English. We had worked very hard at the queer words, but now as they sang "We tree Kings" and "Ark! Ze 'erald hangels sing!" words didn't matter any more. They were children singing of the dear, sweet joys of Christmas, and their papas and mamans listened, very silent, very moved—just as in Britain—just as anywhere in the world.

The next morning, when we were clearing up the Salle de Ping-Pong, Monsieur le Curé came over to speak to me.

"Miss," he said, "I hope you noticed it, but I had two helpings of the pudding. And now at last I understand something that has always puzzled me!"

"Really!" I said, very gratified.

"Yes," he said. "I now understand why, over there in Britain, after the Christmas dinner, one tells those ghost stories!"

Examination in Alençon

L ast September I went back to Alençon, in Normandy, for a holiday, and I was naturally delighted to see the heart of the city, the grand old cathedral, the narrow cobbled streets, all look very much the same as they did when I was a girl. After all, what are thirty years to them? They've seen centuries slip by.

I stayed in a comfortable little hotel-restaurant near the Lycée. The Lycée was closed, of course—all French schools are closed for the whole of August and September. So I was very surprised to walk in one lunchtime and find the hotel dining-room packed to the door with boys and girls all about the same age—fifteen or so. And it soon became clear that they had all come to Alençon to sit for an examination of some sort. And that the papers they'd had that morning had been so terrible that they might as well go drown themselves in their soup for all the hope they had of passing. However, they all cheered up over their meat and salad, and by the time they'd polished that off, and a nice piece of cheese, and a bunch or two of grapes, they were braced to face the afternoon, and moved off in batches to get on with the ordeal.

Examination in Alençon

Then monsieur the proprietor of the hotel came over for our usual little chat about the good old days when the franc was worth tenpence; and presently I asked what examination had brought all these boys and girls to Alençon.

"Examinations!" snorted monsieur the proprietor. "My poor madame, you must know that today we are examination-crazy in France. Examination for this, examination for that—examination for almost every job except selling newspapers. And this particular one is called the Certificate of Studies of the First Cycle of the Second Degree, and I implore you not to ask me to explain. All I know is that these children have to pass it if they want to train for teachers or go into some of the branches of our civil service."

And he went on to tell me that the examination would take two days, the written part that day, the oral the next day. And as it was too far for many of the children to go home they would be sleeping at the hotel that night. "We make very special terms," said monsieur the proprietor. "And you saw how they can eat! Examinations don't cut the appetite—not at that age. Wait till tonight though! You will be able to tell by their faces who has passed and who has failed. Oh yes, they'll know. The results always come out a couple of hours after the exam. And a good thing too. Who wants to be kept in suspense? Besides, they *have* to know, since only those who have passed the written exam today can take the oral tomorrow."

It certainly was easy to spot the winners that evening.

They positively shone, beaming all over their faces, and kindly striving to cheer up the "also-rans". On the next table to me, a certain Marie-Louise, who had been the life and soul of her party at lunch, now wept artistically into her pocket-handkerchief—but only between the courses though, because a meal is a meal, and you have to pay for it even if you have failed an exam, so a girl might as well eat it and keep her strength up.

Then monsieur the proprietor came over to my table again.

"Listen, madame," he said, "as you're so interested, why don't you go tomorrow and see Part Two of the exam for yourself? Oh yes, it is quite public. Anyone may go. I may look in myself if I have a moment."

Imagine me then the next afternoon in the large sunny courtyard of the Lycée—waiting with a great crowd of boys and girls who all seemed to be carrying a thin flat book and a printed form. "Oh this?" said one of the boys. "This is my scholar's book", and he opened it and invited me to have a look. It was his school-record and not altogether a complimentary one either—far too chatty in class, I gathered. And the printed form was a kind of identity card giving name, age, address and so on, together with a brief summing-up of all the work done during the last year together with the marks gained and a very candid comment or two by the head-teacher. But what really interested me was the photograph, obviously a recent one, stuck on the top of this form. "But, of course," exclaimed the boy. "We all have to stick on a photo . . . to show we are really ourselves. Otherwise, don't you see, madame, a dishonest type might get his clever cousin or some-body to come along and sit this exam for him."

At this moment a couple of gentlemen came out. One climbed on an old table and began to call out names from a long list. And one by one the boys and girls pushed their way forward and handed their forms to the other gentleman, who looked first at the photo and then at them—obviously making sure they were really themselves and not some clever "stand-in". When they'd all been checked over, we moved slowly into the Lycée, up a flight of stone steps and into a room with a notice tacked on the door: Salle des Pas-Perdus. This is the French for waiting-room, but it really means "Room of the Lost Steps", which to my mind shows the difference between us and the French. We just wait. They pace up and down.

But we didn't waste many steps. Almost immediately we all moved on into the examination rooms. There were two of them. One was obviously the hall, for there was a large platform at one end, on which somebody had spread a handsome crop of onions to dry. There were desks and seats all over the floor, but some of them had been grouped together to make little consult-ing-rooms as it were, each with a large notice pinned on the walls: History, or Geography or Latin, English, Natural Sciences, and so on. And under these notices sat the examiners, men and women, two to each subject.

In less than no time the examination was in full

swing. To my mind, it was as fantastic as holding an examination on the platform of a busy railway station. There were spectators like me who had turned up out of curiosity; there were anxious parents sitting at odd benches chatting to other anxious parents; there were more happy-go-lucky parents who just popped in to see how things were going, and then popped out again; there was a nun in a quiet corner peacefully saying her rosary; there were a couple of workmen padding about in their slippers carting desks about; and there were any number of boys and girls milling round, looking far too carefree to be natural. So I tackled one such jovial group. And I was right. "Ah no, madame!" they said. "We passed last year. We've just come to encourage poor old Henri here."

At that moment one of the examiners sitting under the notice which said English called "Guillemier, Henri Max". And up stepped poor old Henri and was handed a book and invited to sit down at a desk near the examiner and have a look at a certain passage. "I'll call you in a quarter of an hour," warned the examiner, and turned to question another lad.

So there sat Henri, head in his hands, trying to work out his piece of English, with his friends looking over his shoulder and breathing down his neck, but not daring to give any little tips of course, because fair's fair, and, anyhow, these examiners have eyes in the back of their heads.

I decided poor old Henri had quite enough supporters, so I moved on to the next group. And there

Examination in Alençon

was a girl drawing a most peculiar map—no country I could recognize, anyway—and all around her clustered her friends watching her progress with breathless interest. "Ah non," breathed one, "si on me donne une carte comme ça, je suis fichue!" (If I get a map like that, then I've had it!)

Then I heard the examiner in English imploring a little silence IF you please, so I went back to see how poor old Henri was getting on. And there he was reading aloud in English—something very tricky, which I think must have been: They plough the fields and scatter the grain. But poor old Henri, red and anguished, was mumbling: "Zey . . . pluff . . . se . . . fild . . . and scayter ze . . . grans."

"Try the next line," suggested the examiner and put his feet up on a chair and lit a cigarette to steady his nerves.

Oh no, there was no ceremony about the examiners either. They smoked, and cracked little jokes, and from time to time implored the rest of us for a little silence. But I simply had to admire the way every one of them strove to put the boys and girls at their ease, and the very patient skilful way they questioned them.

There was one gentleman in particular who positively fascinated me. He wore a green open-necked shirt, riding breeches of yellow tweed, thick white stockings and a pair of rope-soled sandals. "Ah, Madeleine Labise," he said to a young woman in earrings and the tightest of perms. "Sit down, mademoiselle. Now what can you tell me about Madagascar?"

"Madagascar!" bleated Madeleine. "Mad-a" and gave an anguished choke.

"Ah, ne vous emotionnez pas," said the examiner soothingly.

But Madagascar went on filling Madeleine with emotion, so he kindly changed the subject.

"Let us hear then what you know about Algeria."

And all the friends waiting about Madeleine breathed again as she sat up, patted her hair, and positively poured out a torrent of information about Algeria.

Well, by this time I was beginning to feel my age, so I made for a bench near a window and sat down for a rest. And when I turned round, why, there was Marie-Louise, the girl who'd wept so hard between the courses at dinner last night. "Oh," I said, "so you're here: I'm so glad. I thought you looked a little . . . upset . . . last night."

"Oh, I was, I was," said Marie-Louise. "I was desolated. You see, madame, I didn't pass the written. Papa will be furious, but furious! I've just come along to the Oral to keep the others company. Oo-ooo! There's my friend Paulette going up for her Natural Science! Excuse me, madame!"

And off hurried Marie-Louise and elbowed her way to the fore of the little crowd supporting Paulette.

Then down on the seat by the side of me sank a stout woman dressed all in black, long flowing veil edged with crêpe hanging from her hat. But I knew better than to conclude she was a widow, because French women cheerfully go into the deepest mourning for the most distant of relatives. I have an idea that, once having bought this funereal rig-out, they hate to waste it.

Well, this lady was very put out. "Ah, these boys!" she explained. "Look, madame, that boy over there sitting in front of the examiner in Latin . . . that's my boy. Jules. And do you know what he's just said to me . . . me, his mother? 'For heaven's sake,' he said, 'go away, maman. DON'T stand behind me panting. You're making me nervous!' I ask you, madame, me, his mother, making him nervous!"

So I looked at Jules. He was a great gangling lad in a tartan shirt of green and red, plus-fours of yellow corduroy, white socks and very brogue shoes. And presently he came over, with a face like a thunder-cloud to say that he was going out for a breath of air before his Chemistry. And he pulled out a cigarette, lit it defiantly and stalked out.

"There!" sighed his mother. "And he's supposed not to smoke. He gets asthma. But what can one do? They don't listen to their mothers these days, do they, madame?"

I made a sympathetic sort of noise—for Jules, I'm afraid—and got up and made for the next room. And it was precisely the same as in the first one—little groups milling round the examiners; anxious parents here, there, everywhere; a couple of nuns peacefully reading prayer-books; and boys and girls meeting other boys and girls and shaking hands and saying, "So there you are! Tell me, how did you get on with your

History? Now, me, I was terrible but terrible! I assure you, I just forgot everything . . . simply everything. Oh, this is my cousin Paul, from Paris. He's here on holiday, so he came to give me his moral support, hein, Paul?"

At this, I edged my way towards Paul and politely asked him a question or two. "Oh yes, madame," said Paul, "it's precisely the same in Paris—all over France, in fact. It's fun in a way . . . if you pass, that is, of course."

"Fun!" groaned a voice. And there was Jules's mother standing at my elbow. So I muttered something about a breath of fresh air too, and hurried out, down the stone steps, and in the dark porch I bumped into a gentleman—also in a great hurry—who gasped, "Tiens! C'est toi, Ernestine?" And I said, no, sorry, I wasn't Ernestine, and, well, one excuse led to another, and presently there we were chatting away on the best of terms.

It seemed he taught mathematics and he ought to have been up there examining away, but that he had only just come back from a fishing holiday to find a letter on his mat saying they'd put forward the dates of the exam. So he was on his way to apologise to Monsieur the President of the Examination.

And this president of the examination, it seemed, was a very good one. Later on he would sit in a special room with a jury of examiners to study the results. Sometimes, of course, it was easy. A boy or a girl passed so brilliantly, or failed so dismally, that there could be no argument about it. But all the borderline cases, the doubtful ones, now they were most carefully considered. Their school records were looked into, all their marks read aloud, their examiners asked to give their opinions, and then if there was still any doubt it was put to the vote.

"But do come back presently," urged my new friend, "then you'll hear the results."

So I decided to go to a pastry-cook's around the corner, the one with "Five o'clocks" written in elegant gold letters on his window. And I had a "five o'clock" —some very weak tea and two delicious cakes—and presently there I was back again, waiting under the plane trees with a great crowd of eager boys and girls.

Suddenly a solemn silence fell as an important-looking gentleman came out, climbed on the table, and proceeded to read out the names of the successful. But what he really needed was a megaphone, for at every name one little group or another started hip-pip-ping and smacking backs and shaking hands and kissing on both cheeks. By and by the gentleman, now quite hoarse, waved a final hand, and climbed down from his table. Whereupon we all decided to call it a day as well, and set course for home—talking, explaining, rejoicing and lamenting.

On a bench under a plane tree, however, I spotted two of the disappointed—Marie-Louise and her friend Paulette. So I said, "Never mind, cheer up! What about joining me in an ice-cream?"

And Marie-Louise said, "Avec plaisir, madame." And off we went.

Half an hour later we were still sitting on chairs on the pavement outside the Café Duc d'Alençon, enjoying ice-cream and some sticky drink called grenadine. And Marie-Louise was saying, "But tell me, madame, this fog of yours in London, does it happen all the year round?"

"I do so hope it does," giggled Paulette. "It must be quite wonderful for lovers!"

And they both choked merrily in their grenadine.

And something told me that this Examination of the First Cycle of the Second Degree wasn't going to matter so very much—not to Paulette and Marie-Louise.